THE Paper Airplane Book

THE Paper Airplane Book

The Official Book of the Second Great International Paper Airplane Contest

by the editors of *Science 86*
in conjunction with The Museum of Flight

edited by Allen L. Hammond and Alison Fujino
photographed by Leah Painter Roberts
designed by John Isely

Vintage Books ☼ New York
A Division of Random House

A VINTAGE ORIGINAL,
FIRST EDITION
Copyright © 1985 by *Science 86*
All rights reserved under International
and Pan-American Copyright Conven-
tions. Published in the United States by
Random House, Inc., New York, and si-
multaneously in Canada by Random
House of Canada Limited, Toronto.
Library of Congress Cataloging-in-Publi-
cation Data
Main entry under title:
THE PAPER AIRPLANE BOOK
"A Vintage original."
1. Paper airplanes.
2. Great International Paper Airplane
Contest
3. Paper airplanes—Competitions.
I. Science (Washington, D.C. : 1979)
TL778.P37 1985 745.592 85-91278
ISBN 0-394-74305-9
Manufactured in the United States
of America

Many hands helped make this book.
We owe a debt of gratitude to Dr. Yasuaki Ninomiya
for creating an exclusive airplane design for this book;
we owe an equal debt to Tatuo Yoshida, Eltin Lucero,
Akio Kobayashi, Robert Meuser, Hironori Kurisu, and Yoshiharu Ishii
for generously sharing the details of their winning designs.
We would like to thank Ilan Kroo for technical advice,
Stephen S. Hall for his writing, Laura Ackerman for research,
Susan Williams and Carollyn James for copy editing, Lynn Crawford
for copy transmission, and Helene Ebrill for administrative coordination.
Particular thanks are due AG Industries for facilitating research
in Japan and for agreeing to make Whitewings paper available.

ALLEN HAMMOND AND ALISON FUJINO
September, 1985

CONTENTS

INTRODUCTION

IT ALL BEGAN with a phone call to *Science 86* magazine from the Museum of Flight in Seattle. Would we be interested in co-sponsoring a paper airplane contest? It sounded like a lot of fun. And there was a distinguished precedent: 18 years ago, *Scientific American* had sponsored just such an event. But why another one? What would make it different?

As it happens, a revolution in aerospace engineering has been taking place, with the result that airplanes are rather different than they were 18 years ago. Increasingly, they are not made of metal but of a kind of high-tech plastic. These super plastics are composed of layers and layers of fibers—typically, carbon fibers—bonded together with a plastic resin. These materials are stronger than aluminum, because the layered composition gives strength; they are also much lighter. The combination is making possible many new kinds of airplane designs—longer, thinner wings on passenger planes, one-piece molded bodies on business jets, even wings that slant forward instead of back in the experimental X-29.

We were mulling over these remarkable changes in airplane design when the idea came: Paper is made of fibers, too, usually cellulose fibers. And airplanes made by gluing or laminating layers of paper together would mimic rather closely the techniques being used with real airplanes. What if we changed the rules to permit laminated construction? Would paper airplanes then fly farther and stay up longer? Now *there* was a good reason to hold another contest! And so was born the Second Great International Paper Airplane Contest.

For nearly a year, the ensuing adventure consumed untold hours on the part of *Science 86* and Museum of Flight staff, stimulated student projects and preliminary contests in hundreds of schools, and attracted participants from 21 countries. The contest received international media coverage and led to this book, exhibits of winning planes in the Smithsonian Institution's National Air and Space Museum (which became a contest cosponsor) and in Japan, and much else besides. There were appropriate echoes from the past—several of the winners had also won prizes in the earlier contest. There were even echoes from the world of high-tech industrial competition—Japanese entries captured more than half of the awards and eight of the 10 first prizes.

It all culminated in late May 1985, when some 5,000 paper airplanes converged on Seattle, Washington. Volunteer flight crews—pilots and engineers from the local chapter of the American Institute of Aeronautics and Astronautics—limbered up their throwing arms. And the skies of the Kingdome blossomed with the magic of flight.

The contest *was* fun, and in this book, the official record of the Second Great International Paper Airplane Contest, we have tried to capture that sense of fun (see Chapter One for the story of the contest). And the laminated planes did beat the records of the earlier contest and open up remarkable new possibilities for design. There is another meaning to paper airplanes and paper airplane contests, too, perhaps captured best in the words of a young spectator at the Kingdome, 11-year-old Simon Daughert, who told a reporter from *Time* magazine: "I was going to be a chemist, but seeing all this these neat designs is making me think about aerospace." This book is intended for all those minds, young and old, who like to think about aerospace, whose imaginations soar aloft with the experience of flight, and whose creativity is stimulated by a new design and a few sheets of paper.

Well-designed and well-made paper airplanes are beautiful, in the air and on the ground. At their best, they become aesthetic statements, an art form of their own. At the same time they are engineering triumphs—they fly. Accordingly, we have tried to photograph the winning planes in a way that respects both their form and their function, that captures their beauty and yet displays the subtle details of their design and construction. The result, Chapter Two, is a 45-page portfolio of winning planes to please your eye and and spark your imagination.

And yet, as revealing as photographs are, they do not tell the whole story. They show only the final product, not how to get there. They show you the plane that stayed up the longest, but cannot explain why it does so. Why do planes fly? What keeps them up? Why are some paper airplanes so perfectly balanced in the air that they seem to soar forever, while others swerve and dip and dive? We have included a short, illustrated primer on the principles of flight, Chapter Three, to answer these ques-

tions. And whether your interest is in understanding how big airplanes fly or in learning how to build paper airplanes that will fly farther and stay up longer, this section explains the terms and concepts that you will need to know.

"If you really want to experience, at first hand, the joy of flight, I believe the most exciting opportunity available to most of us is to fly a miniature plane that you've made by your own efforts. That is why I highly recommend that you make and fly your own paper airplanes." So says Dr. Yasuaki Ninomiya, honored in Japan as the true *sensei* or master of paper airplane design. And Chapter Four is designed to help you master the craft and build paper airplanes that *really* fly. Here you will find a complete do-it-yourself kit: plans for an exclusive design created by Dr. Ninomiya for this book, along with seven winning designs from the Second Great International Paper Airplane Contest, complete with templates and detailed instructions. Here also you will find tips on test flying and tuning your airplanes and on the materials and tools for building them. And tucked just inside the back cover of the book you will even find three sheets of the remarkable Japanese Whitewings paper. Specially created for competition-level paper airplane construction, and never before sold in this country, Whitewings paper is lightweight and yet unusually stiff, with the remarkable property of holding the shape it is bent to.

Whether you are a novice or an experienced paper airplane builder, whether you want to replicate the designs included here or just let them and the other planes pictured in this book inspire your own creativity, you will find plenty to challenge you, to stretch your mind and improve your technique. And let no one tell you that what you are making is *just* a paper airplane; hundreds of airplane designers and aerospace engineers, from the Wright brothers on, got their start by building model gliders of paper and other materials. If it has wings and flies, the principles and the fun are the same.

1.

THE
CONTEST
a celebration of flight

NO BRANCH OF the paper family was ignored: corporate stationery, vellum, index cards, cardboard, and onionskin; toilet paper, computer paper, construction paper, tracing paper, and company newsletters. There were five-ring and three-ring notebook paper airplanes, yellow legal pad airplanes, milk-carton paper airplanes, and cigarette rolling paper airplanes. One scofflaw turned the 1040EZ tax form into a plane, and a pilot from Alaska creased several pink "While You Were Out" telephone memos into aerobatic marvels (*if* you followed the accompanying 22-page flight manual).

They came from Yugoslavia and Bangladesh and Saudi Arabia and Switzerland, from 21 countries in all, and bore names like the *Möbius* (with wings to match), the *Spirit of St. Louis* (one of 343 entries from Japan), *Simplicity 9*, and *Trail of Terror, Phase II*. There was the nimble *Fox River Hellcat* and the lumbering *Lucky Lubert*, both versions of your standard paper airplane (known among pros as a dart). There was the James Bond 007 plane, a red sports car with wings fashioned by a Boeing engineer named James Zongker in Wichita, Kansas, and from P.S. 6 in Manhattan came third-grader Zlatko Maras' "suppersonic" ZX. Not every entrant abided by the laws of motion laid down by Newton and Bernoulli, but most lived up to the spiritual guidelines of legendary "aeroplanologist" H.G.G. Herklots, the unofficial poet laureate of paper aviation. "A little while ago it was a sheet of notepaper," he wrote with rhapsodic lift and rhetorical thrust in 1931, "but now it glides like the fairest of white birds."

Contest rules

The official rules for the Second Great International Paper Airplane Contest were simple. All entries must have been made only of paper. Glue and cellophane tape must have been used only for bonding purposes, not to add weight. Paper lamination and paper reinforcement were allowed. The contest consisted of four events—distance, time aloft, acrobatics, and aesthetics (entries in this category had to fly at least 15 feet or three seconds)—and three categories—professional, non-professional, and junior (under 14 years of age). The contest was conducted under the supervision of a distinguished panel of five independent judges, whose decisions on all matters were final.

May 24, 1985, 10:00 A.M. The Seattle Kingdome. The finals of the Second Great International Paper Airplane Contest. After two intense days of qualifying rounds, in which the 4,348 entries were assessed—at an estimated rate of one flight every four seconds—the field had been narrowed to a total of 250 finalists in four categories: Distance, Time Aloft, Aerobatics, and Aesthetics. The participants represented professional (aeronautical engineers and the like), nonprofessional, and junior (under 14) designers.

Among the milling hordes on the infield AstroTurf were representatives of the sponsors: *Science 86*, Seattle's Museum of Flight, and the Smithsonian Institution's National Air and Space Museum. About 50 jolly, often potbellied members of the American Institute of Aeronautics and Astronautics, the designated throwers for the contest, received their final instructions, which largely consisted of guarding the planes from the press. Indeed, troops of reporters, camera crews, and interested observers wandered about, including five Japan Air Lines stewardesses of indeterminate but felicitous function who smiled at the slightest provocation. The five judges—a former astronaut, two professors of aeronautics, a toy airplane designer, and the editor emeritus of *Scientific American*—stationed themselves, and suddenly the still air of the Kingdome filled with white birds.

You would think that an arena boasting 153,000 square feet of space, unperturbed by pole or tree to a height of 250 feet, unrustled by wind currents or thermals, 410 feet to straightaway center field, and 315 down the foul lines—you would think this vast ersatz meadow would provide perfectly unrestricted airspace for paper airplane flying. Not so. Perhaps the Federal Aviation Administration should have been invited to be among the official sponsors.

The skies over second base bristled with near misses and fatal stalls, and there were as many cries of "Heads up!" as at a ballgame. Dramatic departures from flight plans occurred frequently, with a few wanderers making U-turns and heading for the reserved seats. The distinguished panel of judges, along with just about everyone else, was reduced to undistinguished contortions to dodge careering aircraft. Each entry was flown three times, and soon everyone became accustomed to the telltale "frtzzz" of paper meeting AstroTurf. It was not unusual to hear a promising takeoff saluted with cries of "There we got a flight! There we got a flight! Watch it . . . WATCH IT!!!" And then, as the plane kerplunked into a television camera or someone's forehead, a timer would glumly mumble, "Forget it."

Only the finest and most qualified volunteers were entrusted with the grave responsibility of launching the planes. As retired Boeing engineer Jerry Baer noted, "I haven't done this since I was a kid, but it doesn't take too long to pick it up again." And with that, the same hands that helped design the configurational lines of the B-17, the 727, and the 737 aircraft gently shepherded an entry into the air. It promptly rolled over and crashed.

Although some entrants complained that they should have been allowed to fly their own creations, the volunteer fliers were hardly aerodynamic slouches. You could hear them chatter about wing loading, aspect ratios, trim, lift, drag, and dihedrals. They complied with the bewilderingly various instructions accompanying individual planes—from "A wee bit of force" to "Throw as you would a javelin" to "Put your index finger over the 'K' and your middle finger over the 'B' with the thumb going underneath and on the penciled circle." Sometimes they were observed breathing heavily on the tail surface to improve flight, a technique not even Boeing has perfected to date.

This was serious business, of course. The question hovering over the contest was whether any aerodynamically revolutionary designs would emerge from the minds and hands of kitchen table engineers. The contest, after all, permitted the use of glue and laminated construction to reflect recent trends in airplane design. Did it make a difference? As the flights continued, the verdict that

Judge
MICHAEL COLLINS was a test pilot and became one of the original Apollo astronauts. He piloted the *Gemini 10* mission, became the third American spacewalker, and piloted the command module for the historic *Apollo 11* mission, remaining in lunar orbit while Neil Armstrong and Buzz Aldrin became the first men to walk on the moon. He is also the former director of the National Air and Space Museum, the recipient of many aeronautic awards and decorations, and now runs his own aerospace consulting agency.

seemed to be gradually emerging was yes.

As entries in the Time Aloft category wheeled with unseemly haste to the ground, Sheila E. Widnall, professor of aeronautics and astronautics at the Massachusetts Institute of Technology, was asked if any common properties contributed to outstanding flight duration. She wasn't quite sure that the contest gave evidence of any. The strategies, she noted, ranged from conventional airplanelike designs that made slow, hiccupy descents to odd-shaped, disembodied wings that fluttered earthward "like a leaf."

It was those unconventional designs that most fascinated the retired engineers. "A lot of these entries break the mold, and some of them are good," observed Tom Holgate, a former Boeing aerodynamics expert who helped design the B-52 bomber. "So you have to figure out the reason why." He picked up a bright orange object folded out of glossy paper. It had already survived a run through a typewriter, because the instructions— "Launch almost as hard as you would throw a baseball"—were neatly typed on the wings, and there was even a finger hole in the fuselage. "It flies well, and no one knows the reason," said Holgate almost incredulously. "It flies with no visible means of support!"

Tom Holgate didn't know it, but that enigmatic plane that so defied the airspace of his ratiocination happened to be the winner of the Time Aloft/ nonprofessional category in the First Great International Paper Airplane Contest, sponsored by *Sci-*

Judge
ILAN KROO is assistant professor of Aeronautics and Astronautics at Stanford University and a research consultant at NASA's Ames Research Center. He is also a noted hangglider pilot. His research deals with analysis and design of unconventional aircraft, including an oblique wing design known as the "scissor wing" for which NASA built a supersonic prototype.

entific American back in 1967. And its designer, marketing rep Jerry Brinkman of Bellbrook, Ohio, sitting in the third-base box seats of the Kingdome, looked like a pilot who'd just discovered a hole in his parachute. His 18-year reign as a top-dog paper airplane designer appeared seriously in jeopardy.

The 1967 contest, it should be noted, took homemade airplanes out of the hands of classroom hooligans and office ne'er-do-wells, giving them a respectability unmatched since Leonardo da Vinci doodled them in his notebooks. Organized by a San Francisco advertising agency, the competition was announced with a cheeky full-page ad in the *New York Times* on December 12, 1966, and coincided with a raging national debate on the relative merits of constructing supersonic airplanes. On the wings of topicality, whimsy, and sheer fun, the contest soared into public consciousness. It generated such tremendous interest that the entry deadline had to be moved back to accommodate 11,851 entries from 28 countries. On February 14, 1967, the finals were held in the New York Hall of Science. In addition to Brinkman's award-winning 9.9-second performance, the Time Aloft/professional winner came home in 10.2 seconds, while in the Distance category, the professional winner traveled 58 feet, two inches, and the nonprofessional winner went 91 feet, six inches. Would those records be broken in Seattle?

Not by former champion Brinkman, as it turned out. His old reliable flew 9.9 seconds in the qualifying round but swooned to 5.6 seconds in the finals,

well out of the running. With a gracious shrug and game smile, he ceded the crown, pointing out by the by, "I'm sure I could have thrown it better."

Since there were only 29 winners and more than 4,300 losers in this contest, a few words on the *Fox River Hellcat*, a 25 percent cotton-fiber, watermarked dart made by my very good friend Harlan Kingfisher (associates of *Science 86* could not enter the contest, of course, but a little kibitzing and consulting did not seem out of line). The *Hellcat* was patterned on a successful 1963 prototype that flew sufficiently well in study halls to attract the attention of Mike "Bulldog" Vartanian, assistant principal of the junior high school with which the plane's creator was affiliated at the time.

A perfect candidate, in short, for the contest's Distance category.

Harlan also entered the *Humbert IV* in Time Aloft. This model did not really have any rough-edged antecedents designated *Humbert I, II,* or *III,* but Kingfisher reasoned that it was bad form in airplane design not to have worked out the kinks in test models. The plane vaguely resembled the broad-winged Stealth aircraft, which is designed not to show up on radar. The *Humbert IV* worked only too well; it failed to show up among the finalists. Ditto the *Hellcat.*

In fact, they ended up, like the majority of entries, in a vast paper airplane graveyard in the basement of the Museum of Flight in Seattle. There, in row upon row of large cardboard boxes, reposes

thousands of ounces of the wrong stuff. To a greater or lesser degree, they all suffered from the deficiency that judge Ilan Kroo, a Stanford researcher who previously worked for NASA, cited in one plane that, despite repeated launches in the Aerobatics category, made sickeningly swift, lickety-split returns to Earth. "This," said Kroo, staring down at the snub-nosed also-ran in his hand, "requires talents we do not have."

While searching fruitlessly for the *Hellcat* and the *Humbert IV* among reams of rejects, I discovered that many of the failed or disqualified species nonetheless had a special charm and ingenuity all their own.

Bill Wegener of Des Moines, Iowa, created what he called a zeppelin hybrid, which came complete with a balloon, stabilizers, a rudder, clay (for ballast), and the "Tendency to explode like the Hindenburg!!!" Funeral parlor employee Jeff Brown of Seattle entered the much discussed *Flying Lizard*, a green papier-mâché creature of admirable wingspan and ambiguous inspiration; the face and features resembled certain characters perched on the parapet of Notre-Dame in Paris, though, and contest organizers were requested to "Feed two small rodents daily" (tiny origami birds were found to be a satisfactory dietary substitute).

Richard Baccato of White Plains, New York, designed a beautiful number called *Scherzo*, proving that with the right amount of imagination even grand pianos can become airborne. And out of Wayne, Pennsylvania, came the *Beercan Bomber*, constructed out of a Miller Lite beer can and weighted down by this under-the-wing doggerel: "So do your damnedest, wrack your brain, then cut and snip and glue/ We'll make one better from a can from which we've quaffed the brew." If the metal hadn't disqualified it, observers agreed, the bad poetry would have.

Aspiring designers represented different professions, different degrees of obsession, and—as the notes that accompanied many entries suggested—different plateaus of literacy. There was the science teacher from Mishawaka, Indiana, who wrote, "These enterants [sic] are from the 8th grade science classes," and the 10-year-old lad from Bangladesh who entered as a professional—his profession, clarified in an accompanying letter, being "school boy." We learned from a magazine in Italy that Italians had turned their backs on the legacy of Leonardo ("Herewith enclosed," they wrote, "you will find the only two paper planes we received from our readers"). But to compensate, there was the bubbling genius of 15-year-old Ben Waggoner of Lafayette, Louisiana, who submitted 22 designs "developed very recently (in fact, nos. 19, 20, and 14 were developed and folded roughly one hour ago . . .)." A note from M. Long of Cheney, Washington, urged us to "Tell Boeing I am working on a trans-atmosphereic veical [sic]" and the pessimistic Mark Lenard of Durant, Oklahoma, requested, " . . . if I lose, do the honorable [sic] thing." Taped to the note was a match.

For anyone who thinks that following the instructions was a piece of cake, consider this missive from Steva Grbić of Belgrade, Yugoslavia: "J am sending to You mine model of paper plane SG-1,

made of a sleet of paper—format B 5, and his way of making. On the ocassion of his puting in to the air, SG-1 is holding for a puselage on the place marked with letter 'X'. Between puselage and wings must be an angle of 90 degrees."

As in any contest, there were a few entries not entirely in keeping with the spirit of the affair. Along with the usual paper-plate flying saucers, there was a golf-ball-sizcd sphere of laminated paper and one solid, square block consisting of several memo pads glued together. "I don't think these are airplanes," declared judge Dennis Flanagan, editor emeritus of *Scientific American*. "They fly all right, but so do baseballs." And after all, the contest was being held in . . . well, never mind.

For nearly three hours, the wild blue yonder—or as close as it gets in a domed stadium—glittered with white and yellow and red paper wings. One pair belonged to the huge *Lucky Lubert*, the *Spruce Goose* of paper aviation which measured two and a half feet from tip to tail. Designed by Tony Huang of Scarsdale, New York, it went from eagle to ostrich in a few seconds, covering a hair over 100 feet. (By this time it was apparent that the old distance marks were doomed; much more than a hundred feet would be needed to win.) By its third go-around, the *Lucky Lubert* owned an accordion nose which, in the parlance of the wind tunnel boys, was kind of a drag.

Over in the Aesthetics category, where entries had to fly a minimum of 15 feet or stay aloft for three seconds, the petty realities of physics took a backseat to imagination. One retired pilot, inspecting what looked like a flying shirt collar, declared, "There are no aircraft that exist like this, of course—that's why they call it aesthetics." It was a case of art imitating lift, though—it flew passably well and copped first prize in the professional division for Masakatsu Omori of Japan, outdistancing such fanciful competitors as a Superman submitted by Hugh McMahon of Brooklyn (with the cape as wings and a bright blue body), a flying dinosaur *Rhamphorhynchus* by a Japanese piano tuner, and two obsessively detailed F-14 models (a trainer and a combat model) featuring seats, cockpit instrumentation, and even control sticks, by the irrepressible James Zongker, who hand delivered his entries from Wichita.

Longtime paper aviation watchers spotted an omen of things to come when the smallest entrant in the professional Aerobatics finals took to the skies. It was an exquisite origami beauty, two and a half inches long with a three-inch wingspan, black

THE WINNERS

Distance/Professional

First Place	Akio Kobayashi, Tokyo, Japan
Second Place	John M. Green, Huntsville, Alabama
Third Place	Minoru Iijima, Osaka, Japan

Distance/Non-Professional

First Place	Robert Meuser, Oakland, California
Second Place	Tomonori Sugano, Tokyo, Japan
Third Place	Harold and Paul Harrison, Tampa, Florida

Distance/Junior

First Place	Eltin Lucero, Pueblo, Colorado
Second Place	Toshiyuki Sugano, Tokyo, Japan
Third Place	Clint Meuser, Grass Valley, California

Time Aloft/Professional

First Place	Tatuo Yoshida, Yokohama, Japan
Second Place	Tatuo Yoshida, Yokohama, Japan
Third Place	Hiroshi Kaneko, Tokyo, Japan

Time Aloft/Non-Professional

First Place	Yoshiharu Ishii, Osaka, Japan
Second Place	Nobuyuki Kobayashi, Osaka, Japan
Third Place	Hideki Kobayashi, Saku, Japan

Time Aloft/Junior

First Place	Hironori Kurisu, Osaka, Japan
Second Place	Kelsey Walters, Raleigh, North Carolina
Third Place	Phil Atkins, Mishawaka, Indiana

Aerobatics/Professional

First Place	Tatuo Yoshida, Yokohama, Japan
Second Place	Tatuo Yoshida, Yokohama, Japan

Aerobatics/Non-Professional

First Place	Yoshiharu Ishii, Osaka, Japan
Second Place	Ken Schwartz, Chicago, Illinois
Third Place	Gordon C. Fisher, Los Angeles, California

Aesthetics/Professional

First Place	Masakatsu Omori, Fukuoka, Japan
Second Place	Hiroshi Kaneko, Tokyo, Japan
Third Place	James D. Zongker, Wichita, Kansas

Aesthetics/Non-Professional

First Place	Yasutomi Hokao, Kawasaki, Japan
Second Place	Michael Boxer, Erlenbach, Switzerland
Third Place	Masato Okamoto, Wakayamushi, Japan

Honorable Mention

Alan Adler, Palo Alto, California
Bennett Arnstein, Los Angeles, California
Tatuo Yoshida, Yokohama, Japan
Mark W. Ward, Wichita, Kansas
Don and Bob Burnham, Seattle, Washington
James D. Zongker, Wichita, Kansas
Keiji Misaki, Osaka, Japan
Jim Adams, Fraser, Minnesota
Jeff Brown, Seattle, Washington
Richard Baccato, White Plains, New York

Judge

YASUAKI NINOMIYA is perhaps the world's leading paper airplane designer, honored in Japan as the *sensei* or master of this craft. He was trained in microwave physics and recognized as a pioneer in micro-communications engineering, retiring as a senior researcher from the Japan Telegraph and Telephone Corporation. He has been fascinated by paper airplanes since early childhood, however, and has created over 750 original designs. He won the grand prizes in Distance and Time Aloft of the First Great International Paper Airplane Contest (Pacific Basin Region) in 1967, and is the author of a seven volume series, *Collection of High Performance Paper Planes.*

on top, orange on the bottom. Like most of the eventual winners, it came from Japan. Launched with a flick of the wrist, it zipped into a huge loop, rolled over, and then flawlessly circled to the ground. "That's spectacular!" cried judge Ilan Kroo. Dennis Flanagan, who doesn't seem like a man normally at a loss for words, was reduced to a series of "Woo-woo-woo" sounds as this minuet on wings buzzed around his head.

It was a tough act to follow, but the plane's designer, Tatuo Yoshida, provided an even more spectacular encore—what you might call a Chinese puzzle of a plane. It looked like a conventional paper airplane, save for a trailing tail of yellow tissue paper and a tiny paper glider tucked like a piggyback-riding infant in a slot atop the fuselage of the bigger plane. Launched at a steep angle, the mama plane soared to a height of about 50 feet, at which point the baby glider popped out and in slow, precise, elegant circles made its way back to Earth. At that point, the Japanese rout was unofficially on.

Kroo later observed that the Japanese entries "were much simpler, more elegant, less gimmicky, and less baroque in design. Throughout *all* the categories." Another judge, retired astronaut Michael Collins, ventured the guess that "the Japanese may have taken it more seriously. Maybe it's

because they have more experience with paper. Or it may be that they are better in precise little details, are used to working on a small scale." Whatever the reason, entries from Japan ended up sweeping eight of the 10 first-prize awards.

Two nonprofessionals prevented a shutout for the home team. Robert Meuser, a mechanical engineer from Oakland, California, won in the Distance category; his airplane, which resembled a small spear with fins, traveled 141 feet, four inches (Meuser took the Distance prize 18 years ago too). And Eltin Lucero of Pueblo, Colorado, took the junior category with a classic schoolboy design that traveled 114 feet, eight inches; boldly experimenting with the aerodynamics of photocopy paper, Lucero's winning entry had, in a prior life, served as a "Residential Appraisal Report." Many Distance contestants had long but circuitous flights, prompting judge Sheila Widnall to observe, "I think if we could have measured distance in circles instead of in straight lines, we might have had a different result."

The Time Aloft winner traveled in the right kind of circles. Chased by three timers with stopwatches, Tatuo Yoshida's lovely, high-winged monoplane made mellifluous dips and dawdled through turns for an astounding 16.06 seconds, shattering all previous contest records. Yoshida, a professional who entered more than two dozen planes in the contest, won four prizes in all, making his journey from Yokohama to observe the finals worth the trouble. You could tell that it would take time for him to adjust to his newfound celebrity, however—each time his picture was taken, he bowed reverentially to the photographer.

By early afternoon, it was all over. Michael Collins was filmed throwing the prize-winning designs dozens of times, and there was grave press analysis about yet another precious patch of American technological turf overrun by the Japanese. Judge Yasuaki Ninomiya, clearly more enthusiastic about flying paper planes than evaluating them, was off catapulting his superbly crafted Whitewings toy gliders into the Kingdome's stratosphere, and boomerangs (of all things) were espied making the rounds in left field. There was talk of doing it all over again in two years, even as the Detroit Tigers were making noises about repossessing the field for practice.

All in all, everything had gone according to plan, right down to the instructions provided by Manuel Luz and Sharon McDaniel of Sacramento. "Special throwing instructions," read their annotated entry. "Make sure you're having *fun.*"

2.

WINNERS

a photographic gallery

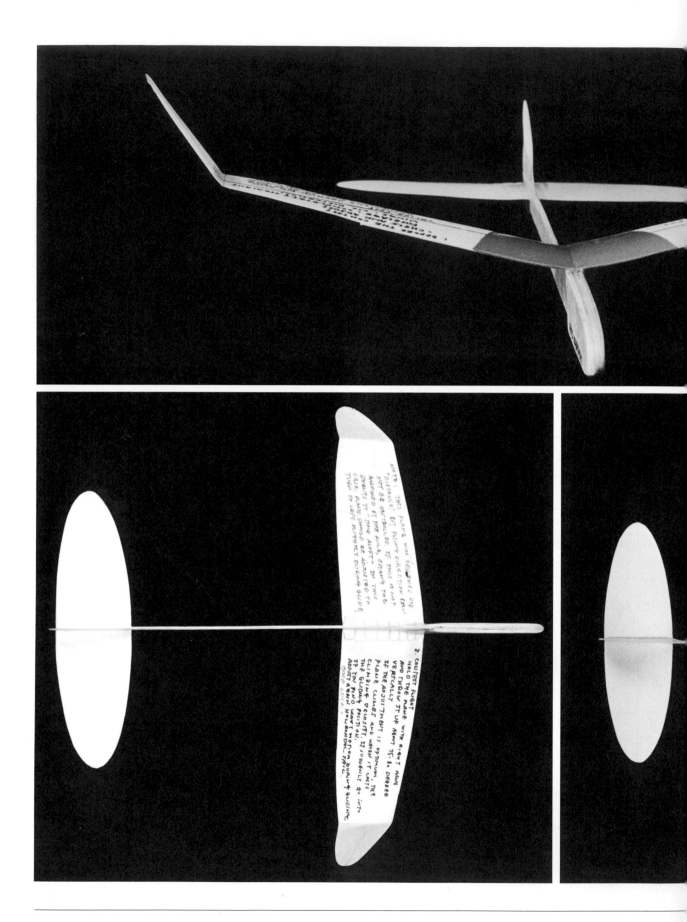

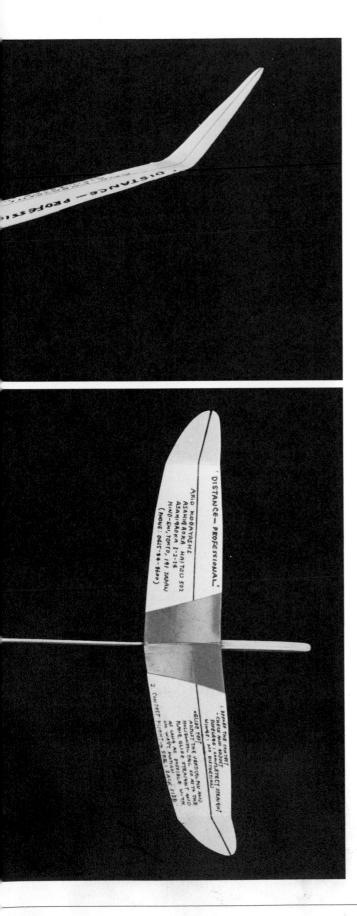

DISTANCE

First Place/Distance/Professional

This plane, designed by Akio Kobayashi of Tokyo, Japan, features a laminated fuselage and cambered wings (the wings have a curved cross section, in this case concave downward). The wing tips are also trimmed radically upward. It flew 122 feet, eight inches to capture its title. Mr. Kobayashi has built paper airplane kits since he was a boy and studied aeronautics in college. He was unable to find work in that field (he works in the research laboratory of Hino Automobile Manufacturer), so he finds paper airplanes "the only way that I am able to work in aviation design." He has designed more than 200 paper planes and spent two months designing and building his winning entry. Because sport fields are so heavily used in Japan, he often rises at 4 AM to test-fly his planes. *Dimensions*: wingspan, 8.5 inches; nose to tail, 9 inches; height, 2.5 inches. **For construction plans, see page 72**.

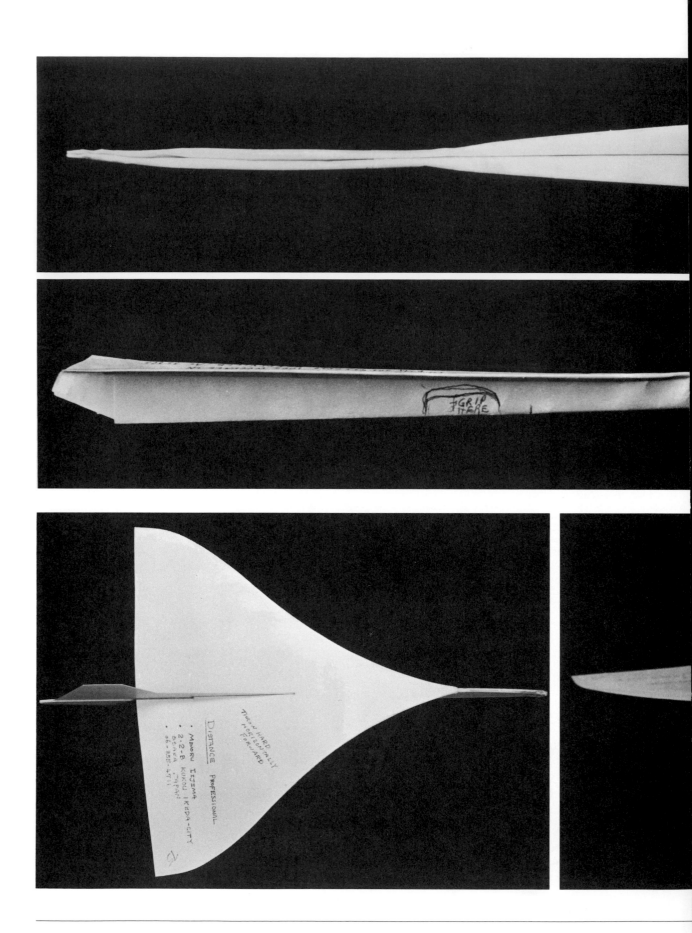

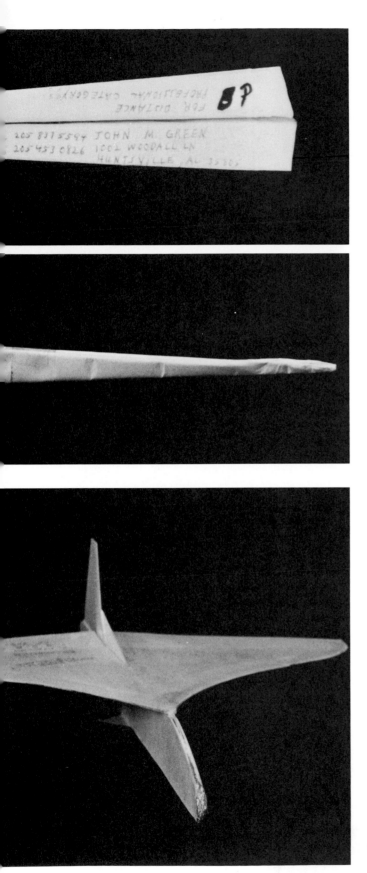

Second Place/Distance/Professional

John M. Green of Huntsville, Alabama, entered this narrow but classic dart design. It gains its strength from several layers of paper with sharply executed folds; the central fold is compressed with tape. It works best when thrown with a strong arm. In the finals it flew 106 feet. *Dimensions*: maximum wingspan, 1.25 inches; nose to tail, 11.75 inches; height, 0.75 inches.

Third Place/Distance/Professional

This SST design was constructed from laminated layers of Japanese Kent paper by Minoru Iijima of Osaka, Japan, and its beautifully shaped main wings feature a subtle camber and a small dihedral angle (the amount by which each wing angles above or below the horizontal). The plane also has a small delta wing below the fuselage. It flew 103 feet 10 inches. *Dimensions*: wingspan, 6.75 inches; nose to tail, 10.75 inches; height, 1.75 inches.

First Place/Distance/Non-Professional

This arrow design featuring a hollow triangular core and three winglets, front and back, flew the farthest of any qualifying entry in the finals—141 feet, four inches. It was designed by Robert Meuser of Oakland, California, an engineer for the University of California's Lawrence Radiation Laboratory. Mr. Meuser has had an interest in model airplanes since he was a child. He has the distinction of having won a distance contest in both the First Great International Paper Airplane Contest and the Second Great International Paper Airplane Contest, 18 years later. His advice to beginners: "The secret to building paper airplanes is knowing how to make adjustments." *Dimensions*: front winglet width, 2.5 inches; back winglet width, 3.75 inches; nose to tail, 13.5 inches. **For construction plans, see page 75.**

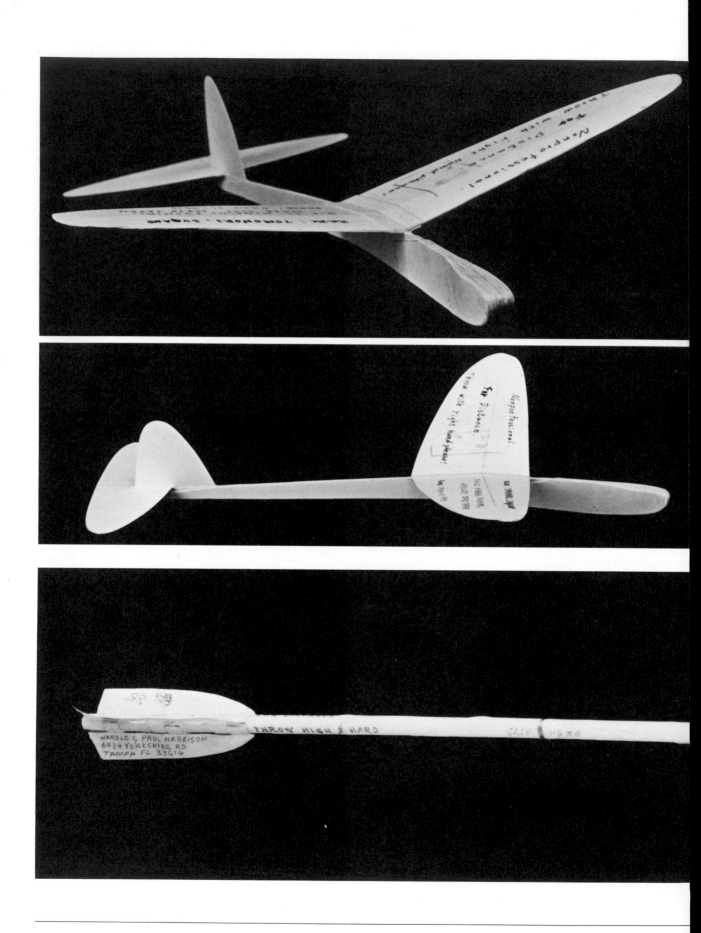

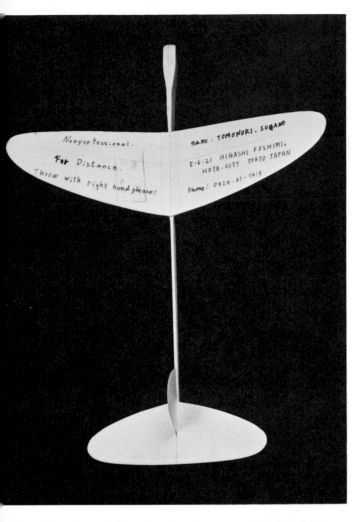

Second Place/Distance/Non-Professional

A laminated fuselage with a fattened, multi-layer nose section and wings sloped up at a dihedral angle distinguish this high-flying little plane. Designed by Tomonori Sugano of Tokyo, Japan, it flew 120 feet 11 inches in the finals. *Dimensions*: wingspan, 5.75 inches; nose to tail, 8 inches; height, 1.25 inches.

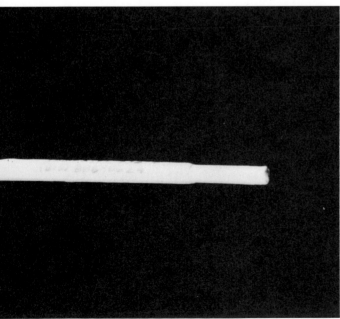

Third Place/Distance/Non-Professional

This hollow-shaft, three-fin arrow design was created by the father-son team of Harold and Paul Harrison of Tampa, Florida. They entered a total of six designs in the contest. This one, their winner, flew 102 feet 6 inches in the finals. *Dimensions*: core diameter, 0.35 inches; fin width, 0.5 inches; nose to tail, 16.75 inches.

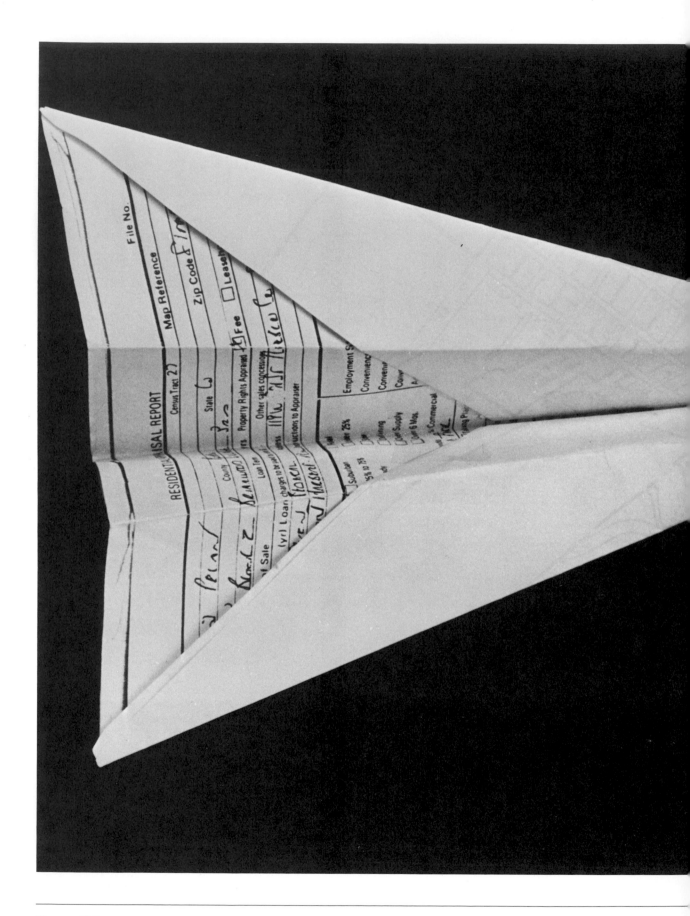

First Place/Distance/Junior

Eltin Lucero of Pueblo, Colorado, created this classic schoolboy delta wing out of a piece of paper that in its former existence had been a photocopy of a "residential appraisal report," whatever that is. Eltin, age 12, is more interested in music than airplanes (he plays first chair trumpet in his school band). He first got involved in paper airplanes when his school sponsored a warm-up contest for the Second Great International Paper Airplane Contest. His plane's best flight distance under his own power was 22 feet, but with a stronger arm behind the plane at the finals, it flew 114 feet eight inches. Says Eltin, "I never thought I would be a winner because I live too far away from anywhere important." *Dimensions*: wingspan, 6.5 inches; nose to tail, 9.75 inches; height, 1.25 inches. **For construction plans, see page 77.**

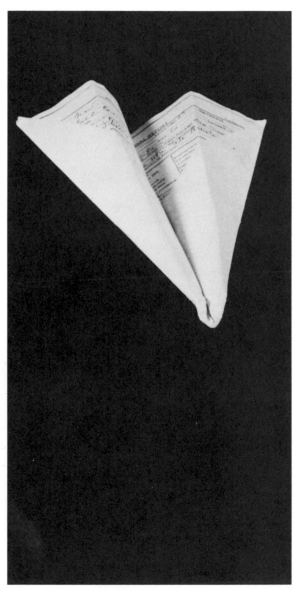

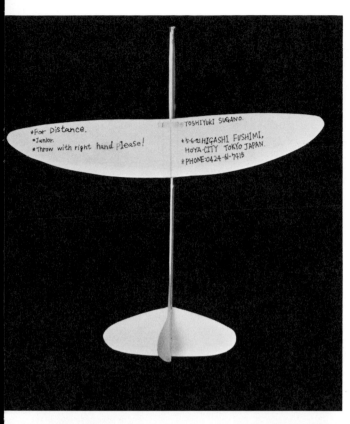

Second Place/Distance/Junior

This sailplane design features lamination in both the fuselage and the wings; the wings also join at a dihedral angle. The design, of stiff paper, is by Toshiyuki Sugano of Tokyo, Japan, whose design skills seem to run in the family. In the finals, it flew 104 feet 11 inches, just 16 feet behind his older brother's second place entry in the adult division (see page 16). *Dimensions*: wingspan, 8.87 inches; nose to tail, 9.25 inches; height, 1.25 inches.

Third Place/Distance/Junior

This conventional dart design, made from white bond paper and with the central fold taped closed, flew 102 feet in the finals. It was entered by Clint Meuser of Grass Valley, California, whose design skills also seem to run in the family; Clint is the grandson of two-time Great International Paper Airplane Contest winner Robert Meuser (see page 14). *Dimensions*: wingspan, 2.5 inches; nose to tail, 12.25 inches; height, 2 inches.

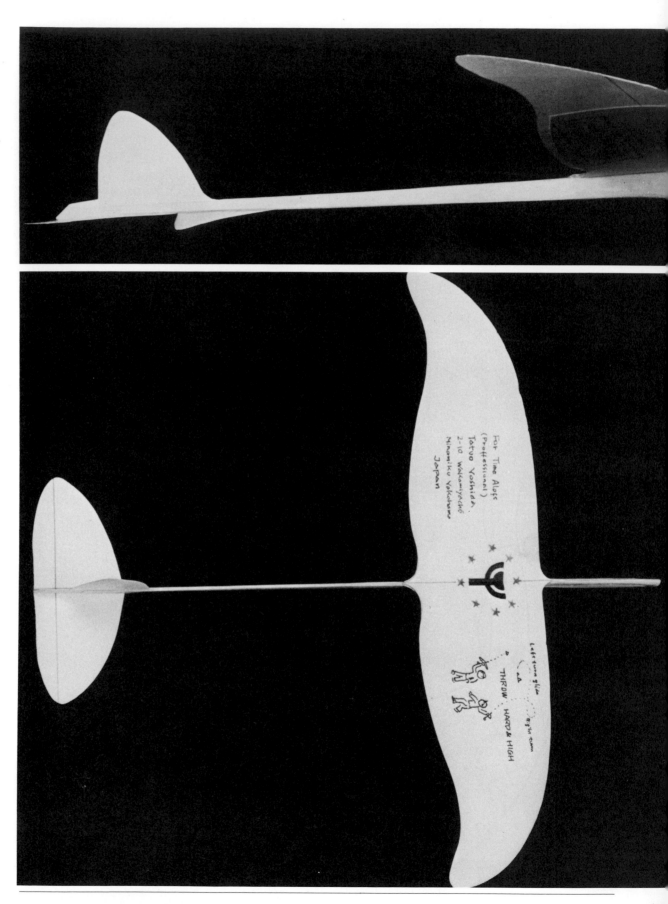

TIME ALOFT

First Place/Time Aloft/Professional

This remarkable plane stayed aloft an astonishing 16.06 seconds in the finals. It is made from Japanese Kent paper and features a heavily laminated fuselage with a built-up nose section and a gracefully tapered trailing edge. The design is the work of Tatuo Yoshida, a professional paper airplane designer from Yokohama, Japan, whose creations dominated the Time Aloft and Aerobatics competition at the Second Great International Paper Airplane Contest, winning four medals in all. Mr. Yoshida has been building and flying paper airplanes for 50 years. In the First Great International Paper Airplane Contest 18 years ago, he placed second in Time Aloft and has twice won the Kimura Cup competition in Japan. "My paper airplanes are my children," he says; he has designed some 500 models and is the author of two books on the subject. For this contest, he entered two dozen planes, refining designs that he had been working on for three years; he also flew to Seattle for the finals at his own expense to "see how my children did." *Dimensions*: wingspan, 9 inches; nose to tail, 10.5 inches; height, 1 inch. **For construction plans see page 78.**

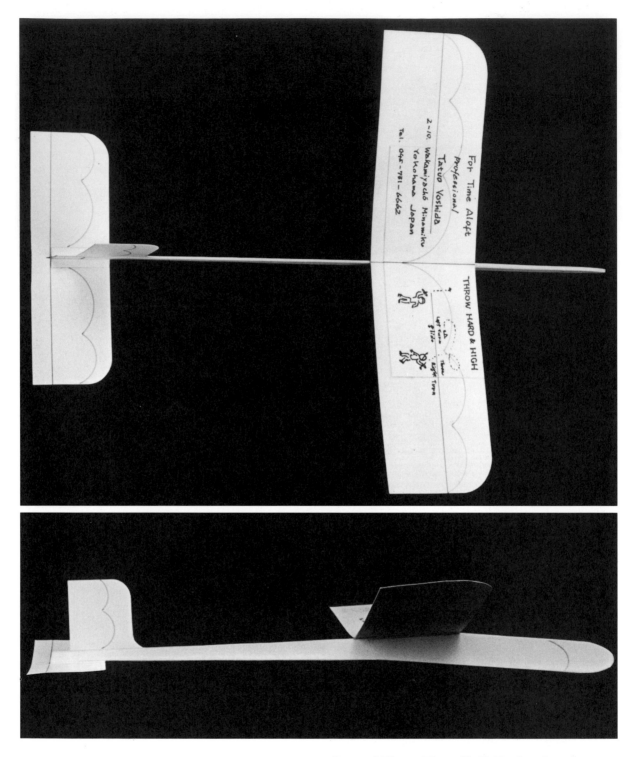

Second Place/Time Aloft/Professional

This square-cut laminated design with wings sloped upward at a dihedral angle is another creation of Tatuo Yoshida (see preceding page) of Yokohama, Japan, and flew for 13.30 seconds in the finals. *Dimensions*: wingspan, 7.25 inches; nose to tail, 9.75 inches; height, 1 inch.

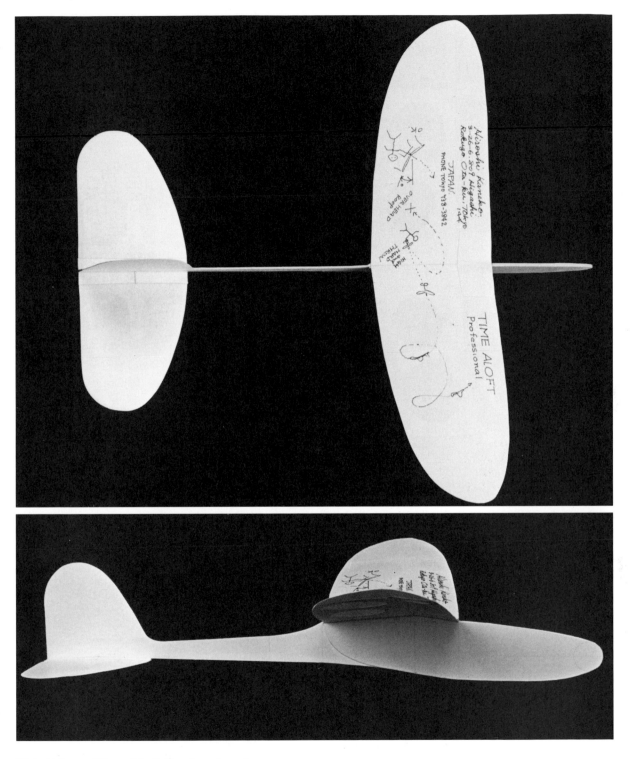

Third Place/Time Aloft/Professional

Wide, cambered soaring wings sloped up at a slight dihedral angle and careful lamination distinguish this design, entered by Hiroshi Kaneko of Tokyo, Japan. In the finals, it stayed up 11.66 seconds. *Dimensions*: wingspan, 8.5 inches; nose to tail, 10 inches; height, 2 inches.

First Place/Time Aloft/Non-Professional

This classic sailplane design features laminated construction with a built-up nose section and a smart decor. In the finals, it stayed up 9.8 seconds. It was built by Yoshiharu Ishii of Osaka, Japan, who also won First Place in the Non-Professional Aerobatics competition. Mr. Ishii is chief fuel engineer at Osaka International Airport, but in his spare time he is a paper airplane enthusiast and a devoted member of a Whitewings paper airplane sport club. He began making model airplanes in early childhood—paper, bamboo, and plastic. Later as an adult he returned to the hobby and now spends about an hour a day building paper planes. He entered the contest at the urging of friends and built 11 entries in about two weeks, to see, he says, "how well my knowledge of paper airplane design would do in competition." He hopes the contest will interest more adults in paper airplane competition because "it is a hobby that doesn't cost much, can be done outdoors, and is good for the brain." *Dimensions*: wing span, 8 inches; nose to tail, 8.75 inches; height, 1.5 inches. **For construction plans, see page 83.**

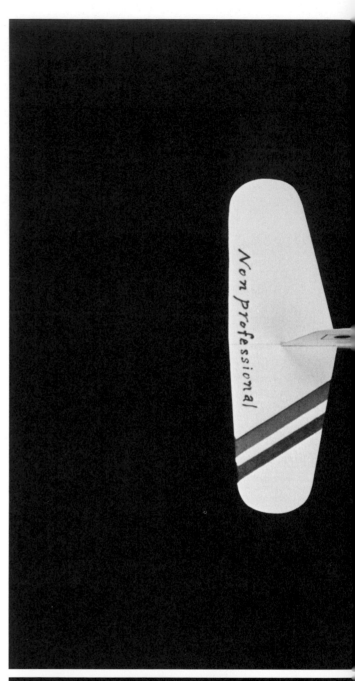

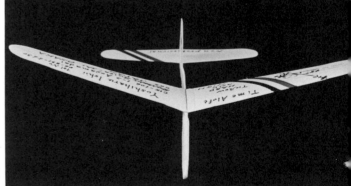

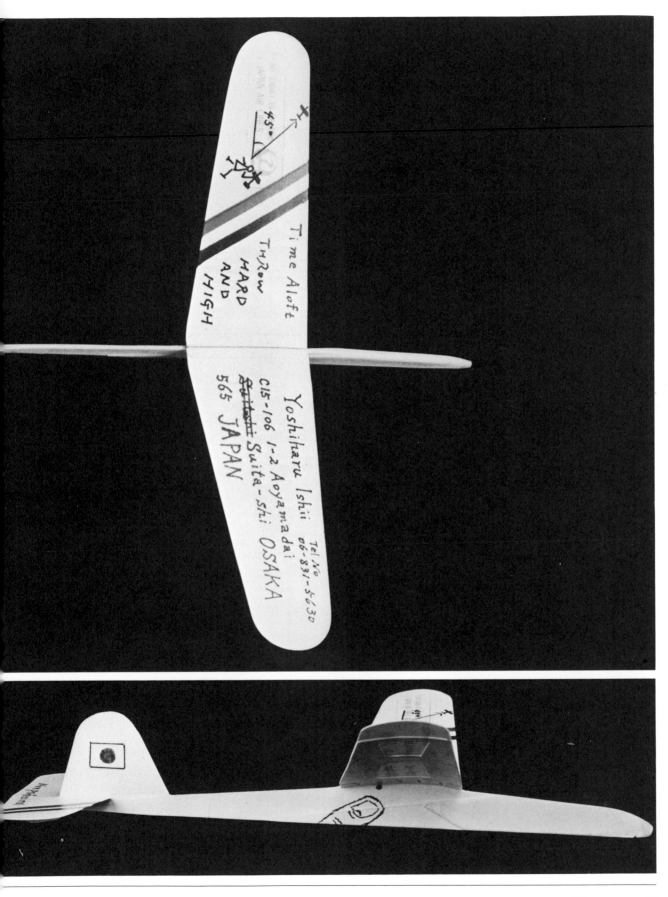

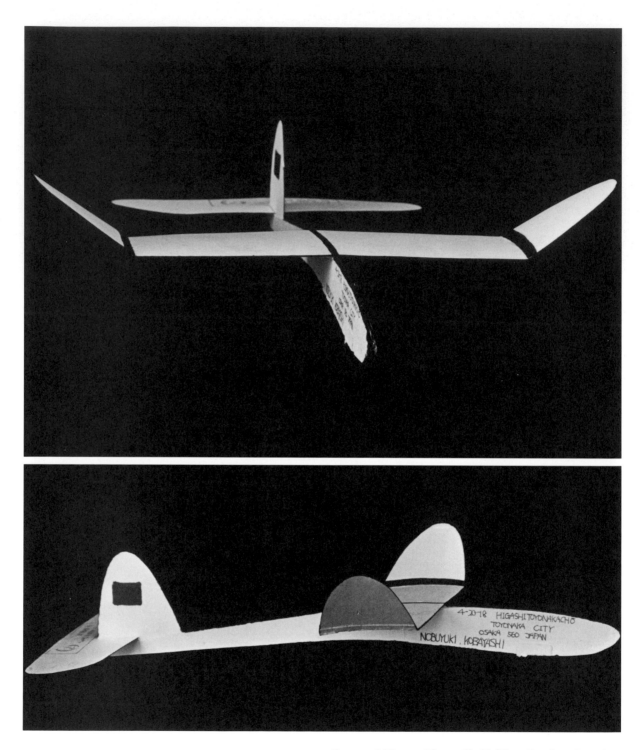

Second Place/Time Aloft/Non-Professional

Nobuyuki Kobayashi of Osaka, Japan, entered this striking design, featuring all laminated construction, underwing cutouts, and wingtips that are flared sharply upwards. In the finals it flew for 9.62 seconds, nearly good enough for a First. *Dimensions*: wingspan, 7.25 inches; nose to tail, 8.75 inches; height, 1.5 inches.

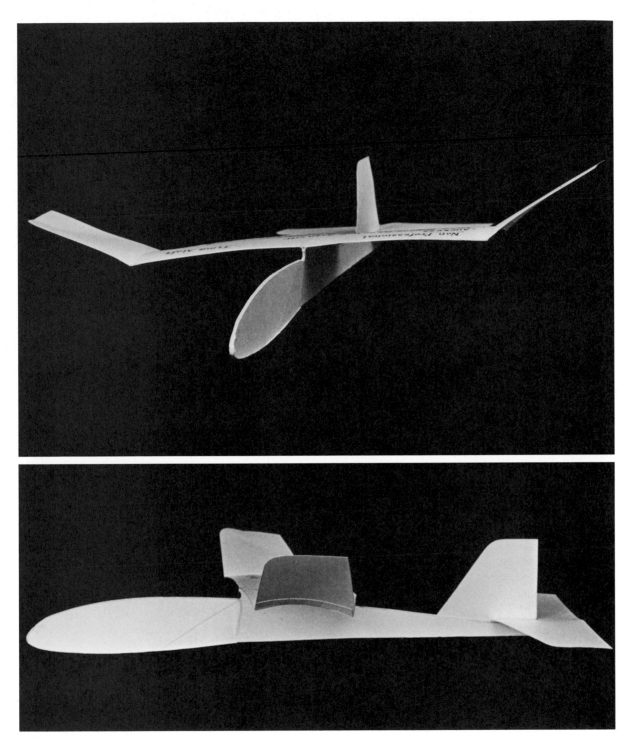

Third Place/Time Aloft/Non-Professional

Flared wing tips, underwing cutouts, and a built-up nose section distinguish this laminated design, entered by Hideki Kobayashi of Saku, Japan. In the finals this plane stayed aloft for 9.07 seconds. *Dimensions*: wingspan, 9.25 inches; nose to tail, 9.5 inches; height, 1.5 inches.

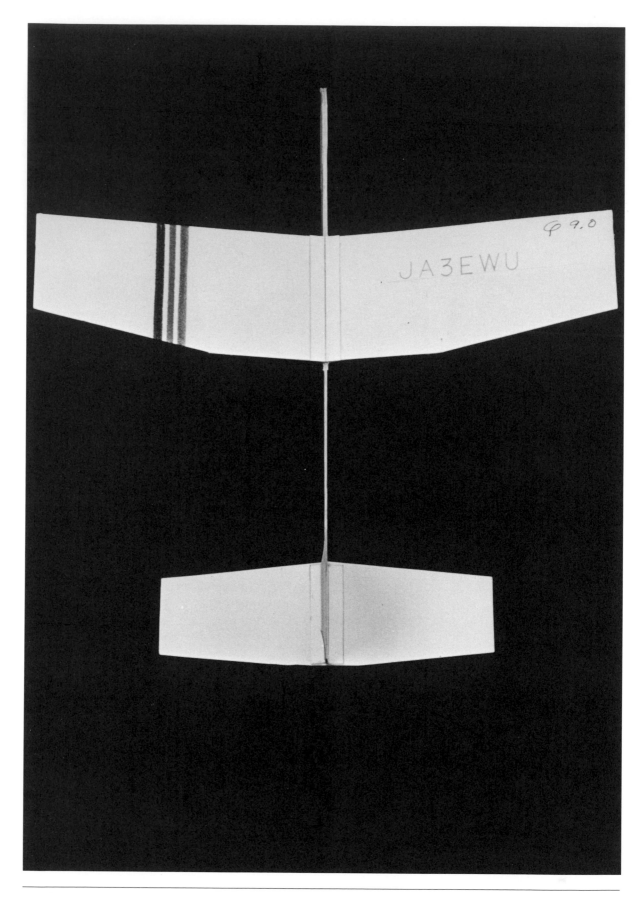

First Place/Time Aloft/Junior

Hironori Kurisu, age 10, of Osaka, Japan, designed and built this squared-off sailplane that performed better in the finals than many adult winning designs; it stayed up 11.28 seconds. The plane, like many of the Time Aloft winners, is of laminated Japanese Kent paper construction, featuring a built-up nose section and underwing cutouts. Hironori is not a newcomer to paper airplane design; he is the youngest child in a family which has been making paper airplanes for generations, and he is an active member of a Whitewings paper airplane club. His aspiration "To build lighter, better looking planes, to be as good as Dr. Ninomiya (see Judge, page 8)." *Dimensions*: wingspan, 7.75 inches; nose to tail, 8.25 inches; height, 2 inches. **For construction plans, see page 89.**

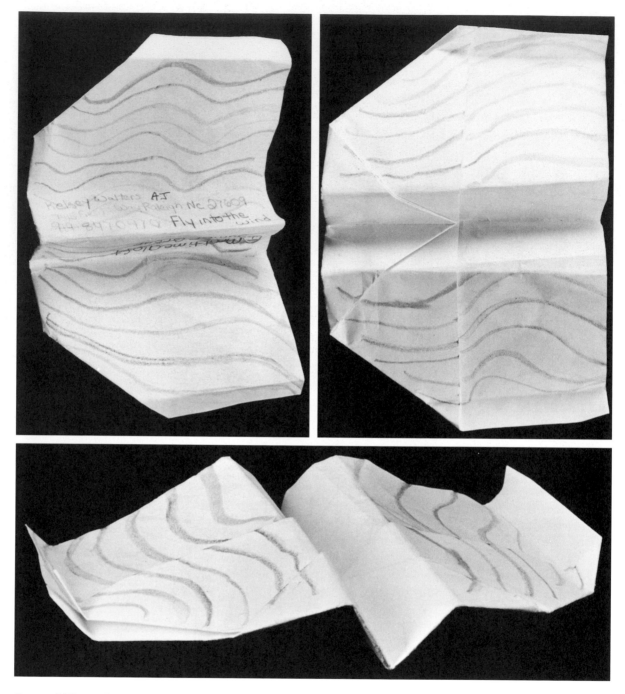

Second Place/Time Aloft/Junior

Decorated with crayon pinstriping, this wide-open flying wedge design features a double-ply leading edge and front section. It is the creation of Kelsey Walters of Raleigh, North Carolina, and stayed up 7.54 seconds in the finals. *Dimensions*: wingspan, 6.5 inches; nose to tail, 4.5 inches; height, 0.75 inches.

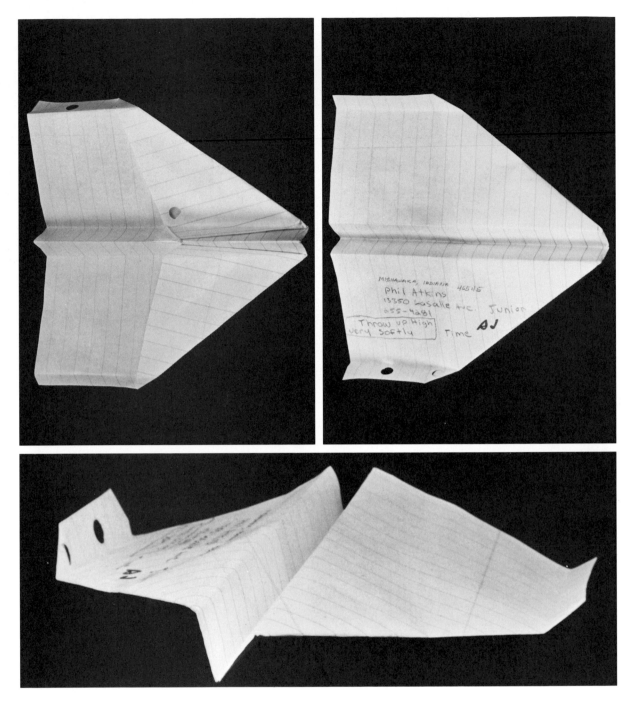

Third Place/Time Aloft/Junior

This plane is a broad and extremely flexible delta wing
design, made of loosely folded notebook paper, with up-
turned wing tips and a two-ply front section. Entered by
Phil Atkins of Mishawaka, Indiana, it flew for 7.20 seconds in the finals. *Dimensions*: wingspan, 7.5 inches; nose
to tail, 6.5 inches; height, 0.5 inches.

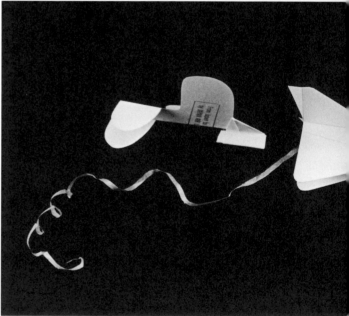

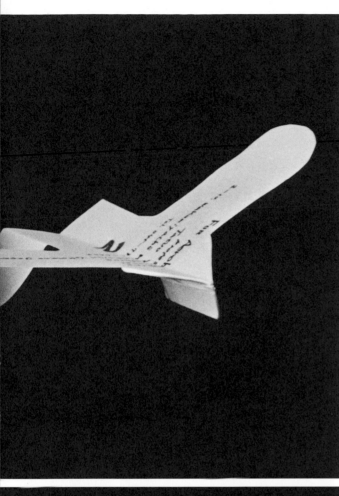

AEROBATICS

First Place/Aerobatics/Professional

This imaginative entry comprises two planes, one piggy-backed on the other. The small plane has a wing with a slight dihedral angle, twin down-turned tails, and a built-up nose; it nestles atop the wings and fuselage of the larger plane at launch, then separates in flight. The larger plane, of laminated construction, features a slotted fuselage and a four-part tail—two angled up and two down. The design is the work of Tatuo Yoshida, a professional paper airplane designer from Yokohama, Japan, whose creations dominated the Time Aloft and Aerobatics competition at the Second Great International Paper Airplane Contest, winning four medals in all. Mr. Yoshida has been building and flying paper airplanes for 50 years. In the First Great International Paper Airplane Contest 18 years ago, he placed second in Time Aloft and has twice won the Kimura Cup competition in Japan. "My paper airplanes are my children," he says; he has designed some 500 models and is the author of two books on the subject. For this contest, he entered two dozen planes, refining designs that he had been working on for 3 years; he also flew to Seattle for the finals at his own expense to "see how my children did." *Dimensions*: (first plane) wingspan, 3.75 inches; nose to tail, 3 inches; height, 0.75 inches; (second plane) wingspan, 5.13 inches; nose to tail, 7 inches; height, 2 inches.

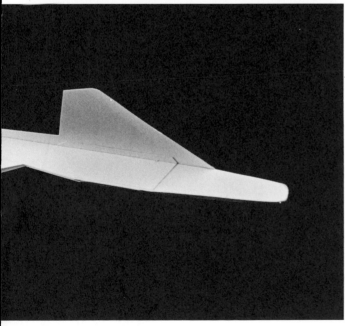

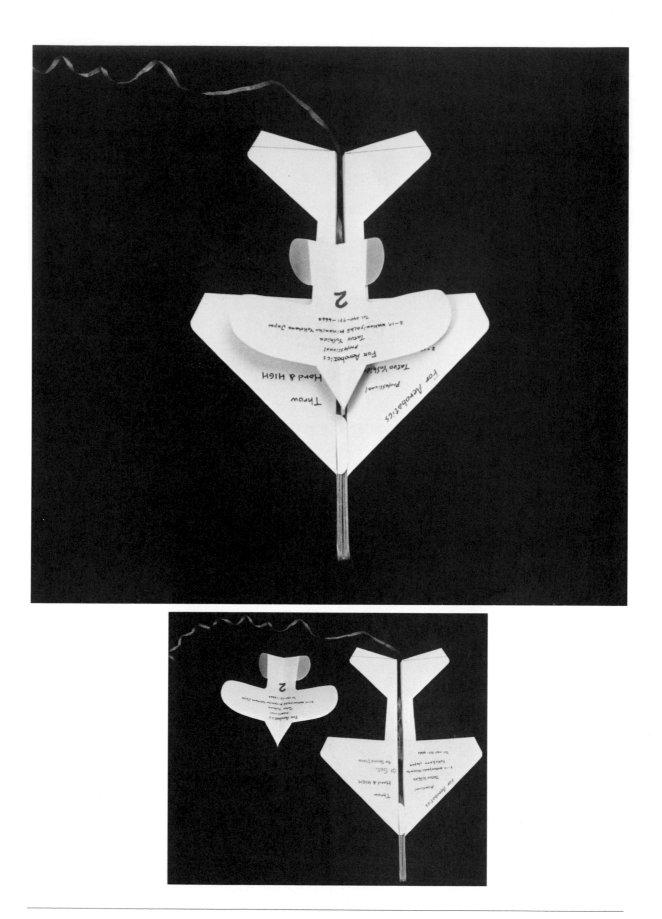

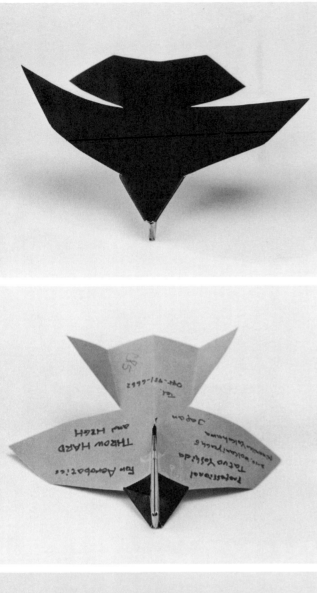

Second Place/Aerobatics/Professional

This exquisite design, also by Tatuo Yoshida (see preceding pages), illustrates the simple delicacy that can be achieved by folding a thin piece of origami paper. Its tiny birdlike shape features cambered wings and twin, down-turned tails; its nose section is strengthened with tape. *Dimensions*: wingspan, 2.25 inches; nose to tail, 2.0 inches; height, 1 inch. **For construction plans, see page 95.**

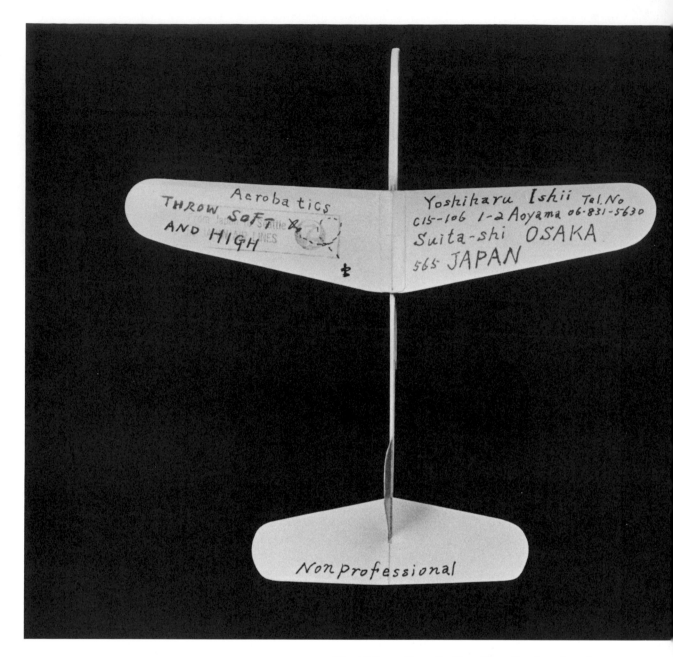

First Place/Aerobatics/Non-Professional

Distinctive in its laminated yellow paper construction
and crisp, clean design, this plane features a cambered
wing (concave downward) which is sloped up at a dihedral angle and a built-up nose section. It was built by Yoshiharu Ishii of Osaka, Japan, who also won First Place in
the Non-Professional Time Aloft competition. Mr. Ishii
is chief fuel engineer at Osaka International Airport, but
in his spare time he is a paper airplane enthusiast and a
devoted member of a Whitewings paper airplane sport
club. He began making model airplanes in early child-

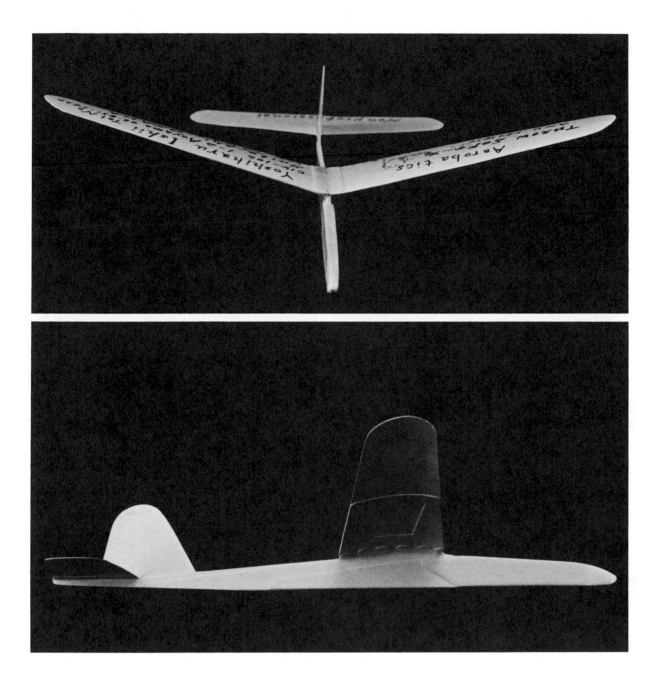

hood—paper, bamboo, and plastic. Later he returned to the hobby and now spends an hour a day building paper airplanes. He entered the contest at the urging of friends and built 11 entries in about two weeks, to see "how well my knowledge of paper airplane design would do in competition." He hopes the contest will interest more adults in paper airplane competition because "it is a hobby that doesn't cost much, can be done outdoors, and is good for the brain." *Dimensions*: wingspan, 6.25 inches; nose to tail, 6.75 inches; height, 1.5 inches.

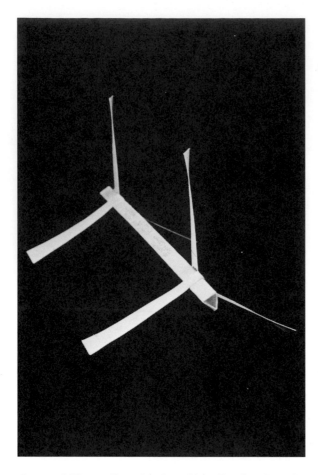

Second Place/Aerobatics/Non-Professional

This unusual entry by Ken Schwartz of Chicago, Illinois, resembles a double-butted arrow. It features a hollow core and three winglets at each end of the fuselage. *Dimensions*: winglet length, 2 inches; nose to tail, 10 inches.

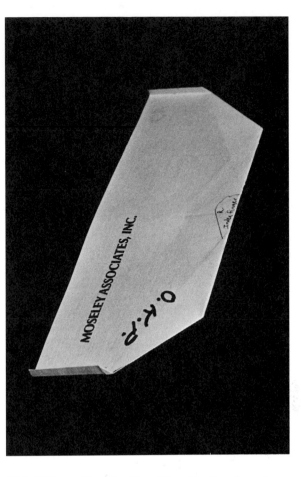

On the plane, handwritten notes:

ACROBATICS

Both vertical
to the wing and straight, front to back.
stabilizers should be 90°
Give to the short chord, performance is relative
to release speed. Hold horizontally, over head, reach
backward then pull the plane forward, release it
when it is directly over your head and snap it
fast for acrobatics, slower for distance.

Gordon C. Fisher
Non-Professional
222. S. Mariposa Ave. #204
LACA. 90004
(213) 837-5945

Third Place/Aerobatics/Non-Professional

Gordon C. Fisher of Los Angeles, California, designed
this highly maneuverable flying wing. It features single
sheet construction, folded to create a heavy leading edge
and down-turned wing tips. *Dimensions*: wingspan, 8.25
inches; width, 2.75 inches; height, 0.125 inches.

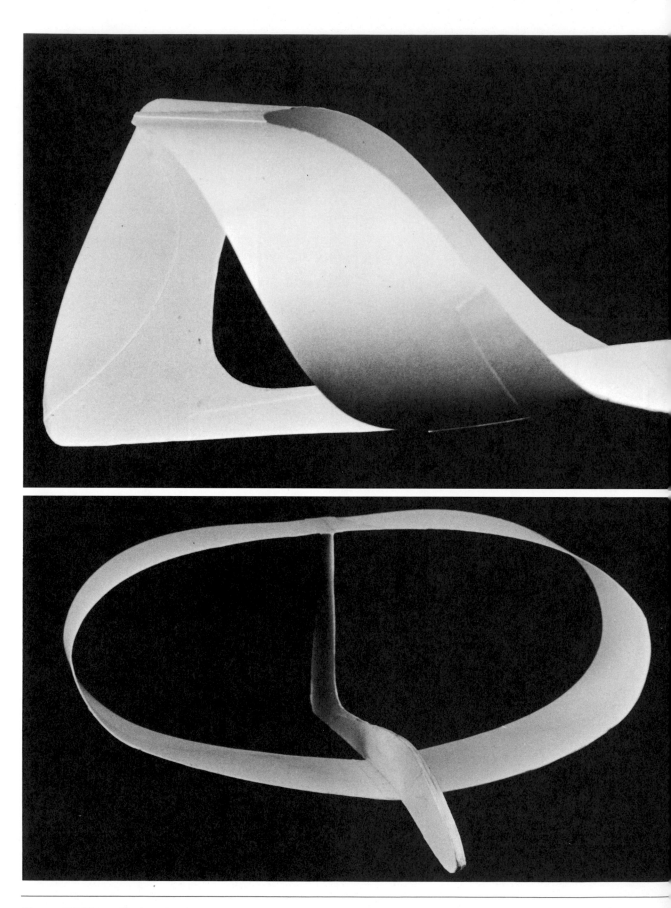

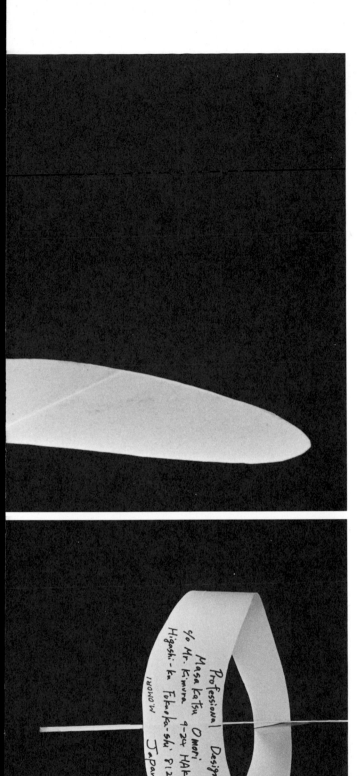

AESTHETICS

First Place/Aesthetics/Professional

This futuristic starship design speaks of the 21st century. Created by Masakatsu Omori of Fukuoka, Japan, it achieves its striking, clean look through laminated construction and features a swept-back circular wing and a built-up nose section. Mr. Omori is a graduate student in aeronautics at Kyushu University where, appropriately enough, he is studying advanced composite materials for aircraft design. His interest is paper aircraft dates back to his school days but intensified when his family was stationed in Iran. As it happened, paper airplane master Yasuaki Ninomiya (see Judge, page 8) was also working in Iran on a microwave project, and he met and inspired the then 12-year-old Omori. *Dimensions*: wingspan, 7 inches; nose to tail, 8 inches; height, 2.5 inches.

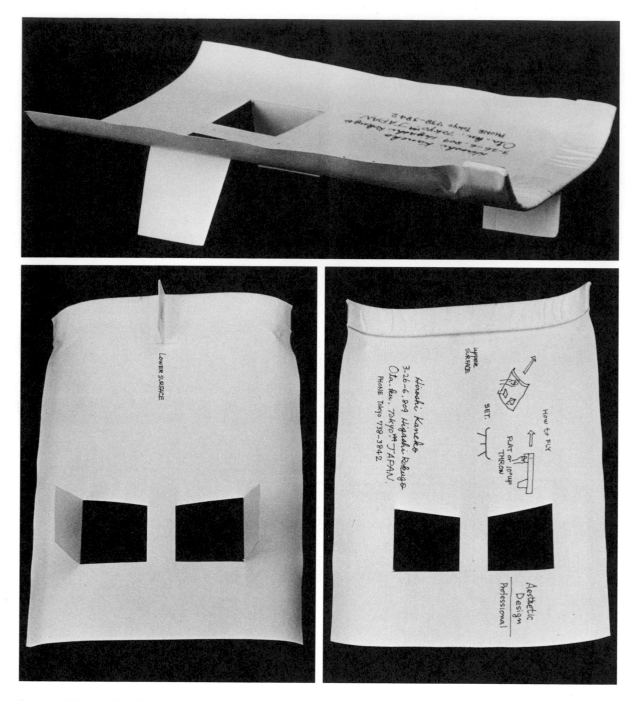

Second Place/Aesthetics/Professional

Hiroshi Kaneko of Tokyo, Japan, designed this intriguing flying wing. It features a subtle curvature to the wing, maintained by a laminated leading edge; a pair of downward turned tails and a front stabilizer complete the plane. *Dimensions*: wingspan, 5.75 inches; nose to tail, 7.62 inches; height, 1.5 inches.

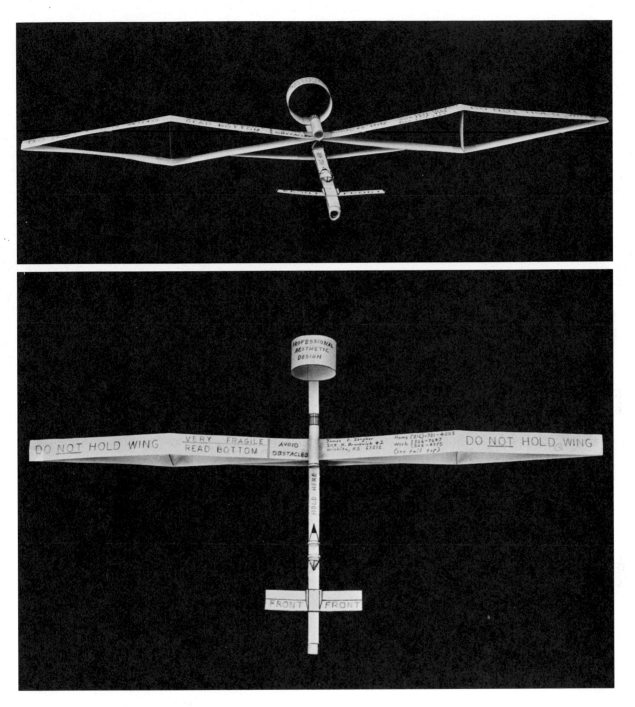

Third Place/Aesthetics/Professional

This elegant and unusual biplane features complex, laminated strut bracing in the wings, wingtips that are joined together, a hollow, triangular core, and a circular tail. Designed by James D. Zongker, an engineer with Boeing in Wichita, Kansas, the plane comes complete with a passenger seat. *Dimensions*: wingspan, 13.5 inches; nose to tail, 7.4 inches; height, 1.4 inches.

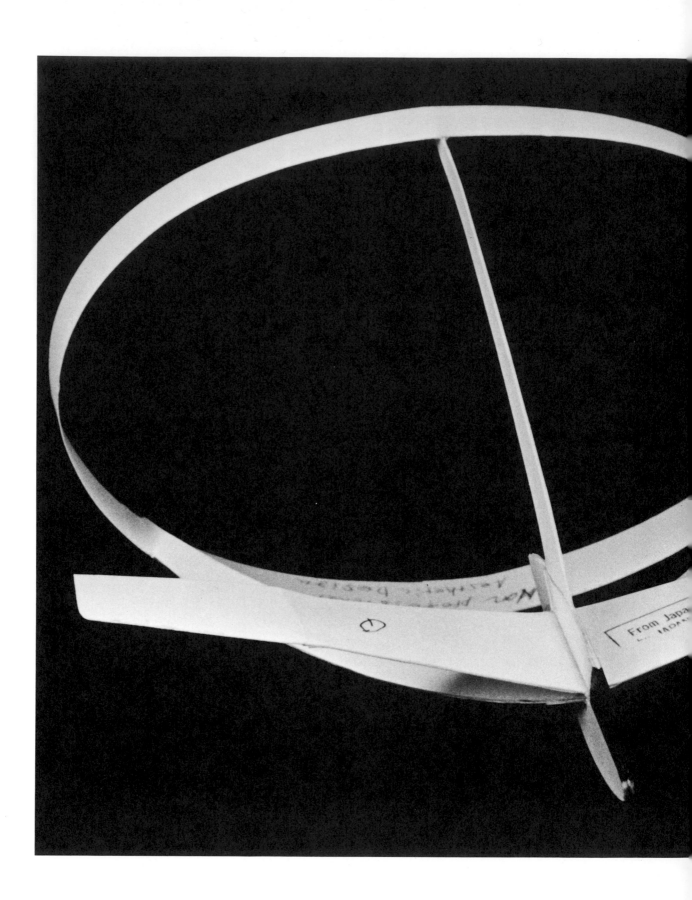

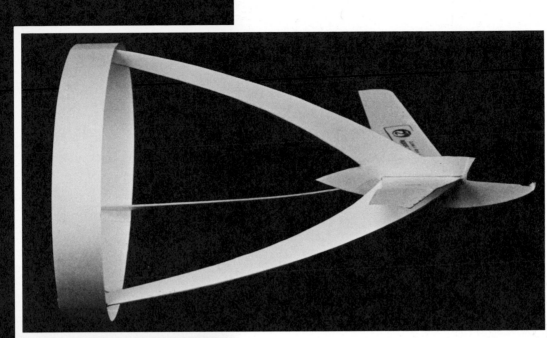

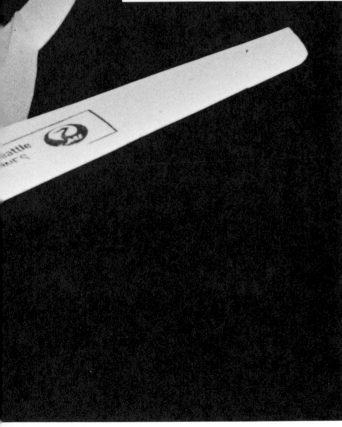

First Place/Aesthetics/Non-Professional

Yasutomi Hokao of Kawasaki, Japan, built this starship design. Made of laminated Japanese Kent paper, it features a front wing sloping up at a sizeable dihedral angle and an oval back wing attached to the fuselage by three curved spars. Mr. Hokao is a student of painting at the Tama College of Art in Tokyo and has also studied the piano. He began a serious interest in paper planes when he won a student contest in primary school and was asked by other students to make planes for them too. He is now a member of a Whitewings paper airplane club and has designed some 200 planes. Of his plane he says, "I was tired of ordinary designs and wanted to do something creative. I also wanted to study the aeronautics of ring wings." *Dimensions*: front wingspan, 8 inches; back wingspan, 7 inches; nose to tail, 8.5 inches; height, 5 inches.

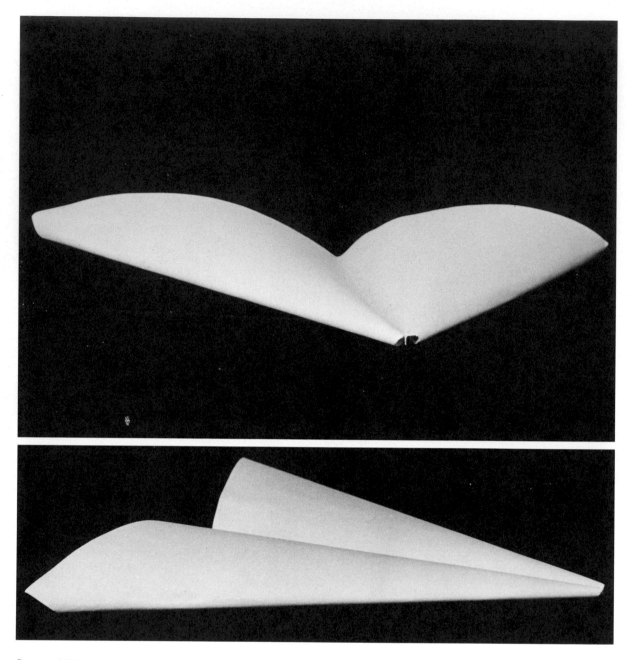

Second Place/Aesthetics/Non-Professional

This graceful design comes from Michael Boxer of Er-
lenbach, Switzerland. It features extremely flexible,
arched wings, curved until they meet in a vertical joint,
with hollow, rolled-tube leading edges; the effect is almost that of a living creature. *Dimensions*: wingspan, 8.6
inches; nose to tail, 9.8 inches; height, 2.4 inches.

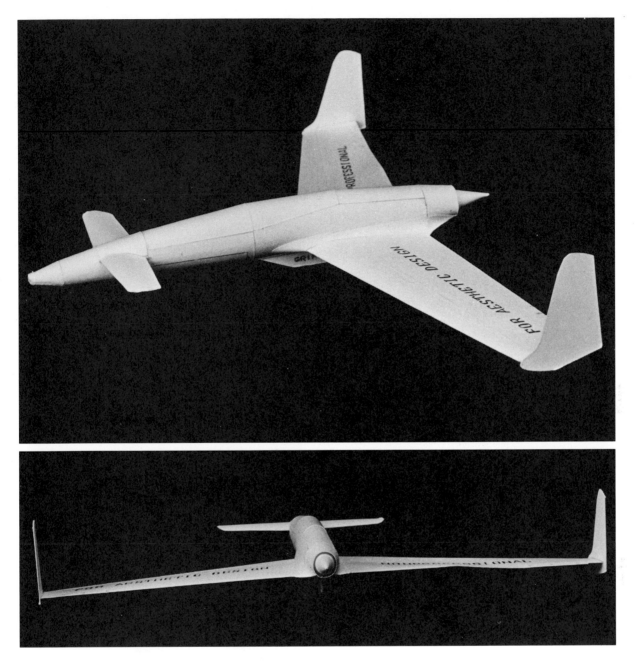

Third Place/Aesthetics/Non-Professional

Masato Okamoto of Wakayamushi, Japan, designed this complex, carefully constructed entry. Its features include laminated, hollow-core wings with airfoil-shaped cross sections (front and back), a built-up hollow fuselage, and exquisite detailing. *Dimensions*: wingspan, 8.75 inches; nose to tail, 6.25 inches; height, 1.25 inches.

HONORABLE MENTION

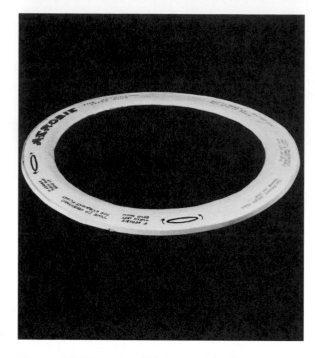

Honorable Mention/Distance/Professional

Flying rings constitute a category in themselves. This one, designed by Alan Adler of Palo Alto, California, flew the farthest of those entered.

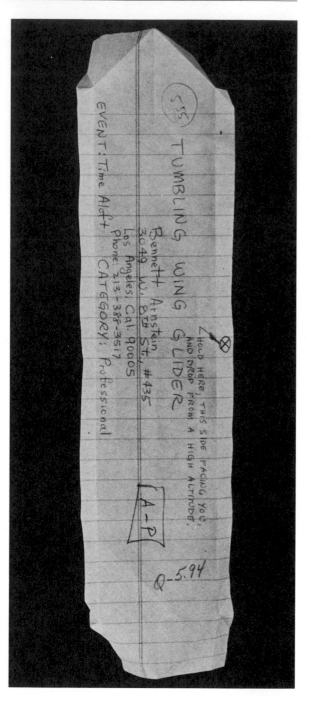

Honorable Mention/Time Aloft/Professional

This tumbling wing glider is the ultimate in simple design: a piece of yellow-ruled writing paper folded for stiffness and crimped at the corners. It was entered by Bennett Arnstein of Los Angeles, California.

Honorable Mention/Time Aloft/Professional

Long wingtips that are bent gently downward and a double downward-swept tail give this plane a striking, birdlike appearance. It was designed by Tatuo Yoshida of Yokohama, Japan, who also won the Time Aloft and Aerobatics competitions (see pages 22 and 34).

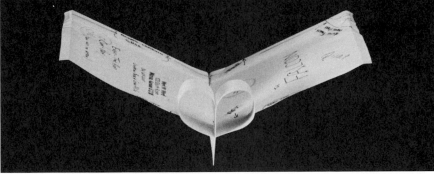

Honorable Mention/Time Aloft/Professional

Mark W. Ward of Wichita, Kansas, entered this intriguing flying wing with folded leading edge, blade-like stabilizer, and an unusual double circle tail.

Honorable Mention/Aesthetics/Professional

Bob and Don Burnham of Seattle, Washington, are a father/son team that built this scale model of a Boeing Monomail, complete with wing rib and skin construction and moving wheels and propeller.

Honorable Mention/Aesthetics/Non-Professional

Jim Adams of Fraser, Minnesota, built this highly detailed model of a light seaplane, complete with propeller, landing floats, and simulated rivets embossed in the paper.

Honorable Mention/Aesthetics/Professional

This intricate "autogyro" design with moving twin rotors and camouflage-colored fuselage was built by James D. Zongker, who also won Third Place in the Aesthetics competition (see page 45).

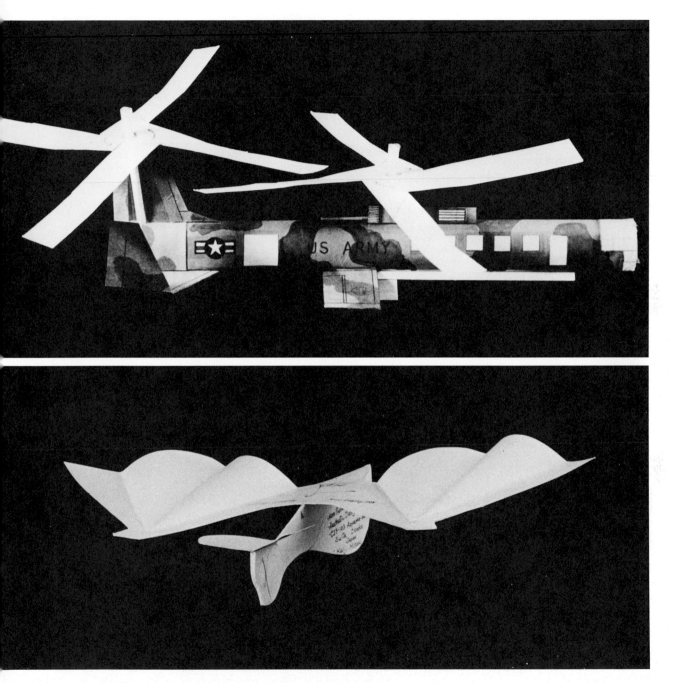

Honorable Mention/Aesthetics/Non-Professional

This plane, designed by Keiji Misaki of Osaka, Japan, captures the feel of a flying bat with its fluted wings and unusual shape.

Honorable Mention/Aesthetics/Non-Professional

This papier-mâché flying lizard, built by Jeff Brown of Seattle, Washington, was complete down to its long fingertips and feeding instructions: "two small rodents daily."

Honorable Mention/Aesthetics/Non-Professional

To show that even a piano can fly, Richard Baccato of White Plains, New York, entered this ink-on-paper design. It did.

3.

PRINCIPLES OF FLIGHT

a sketchbook

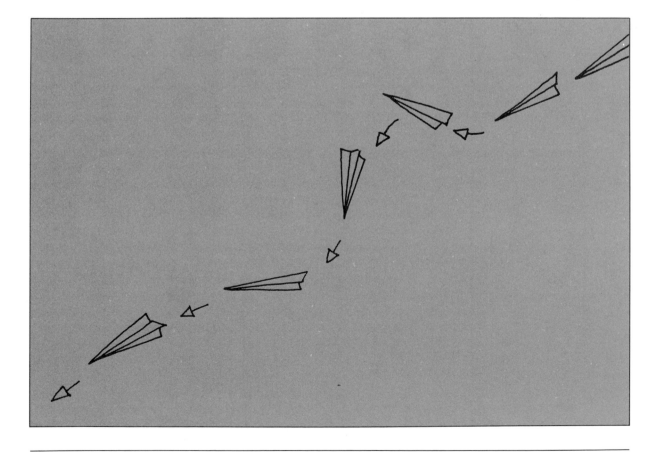

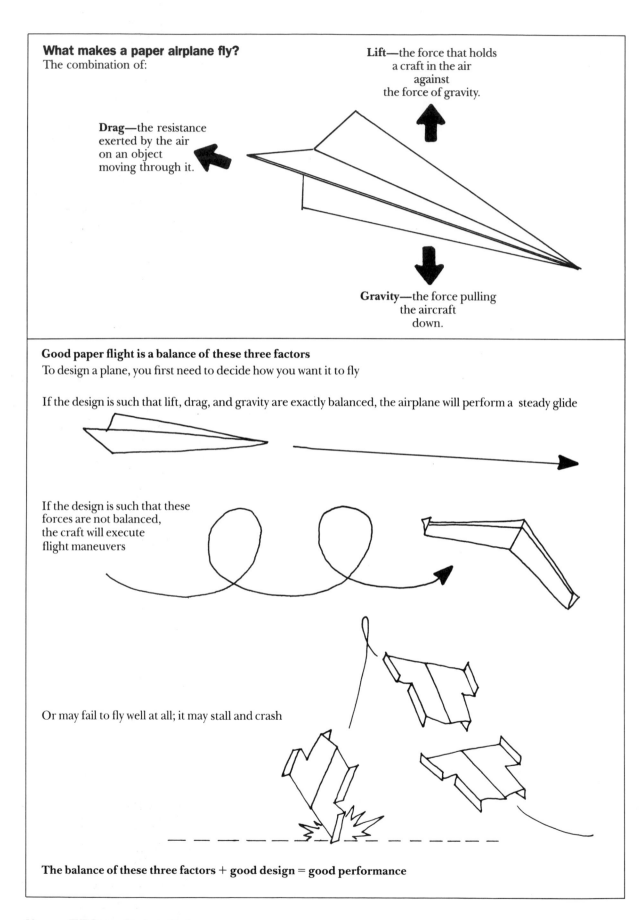

What makes a paper airplane fly?
The combination of:

Lift—the force that holds a craft in the air against the force of gravity.

Drag—the resistance exerted by the air on an object moving through it.

Gravity—the force pulling the aircraft down.

Good paper flight is a balance of these three factors
To design a plane, you first need to decide how you want it to fly

If the design is such that lift, drag, and gravity are exactly balanced, the airplane will perform a steady glide

If the design is such that these forces are not balanced, the craft will execute flight maneuvers

Or may fail to fly well at all; it may stall and crash

The balance of these three factors + good design = good performance

Good design
Almost any paper airplane can be made to fly:

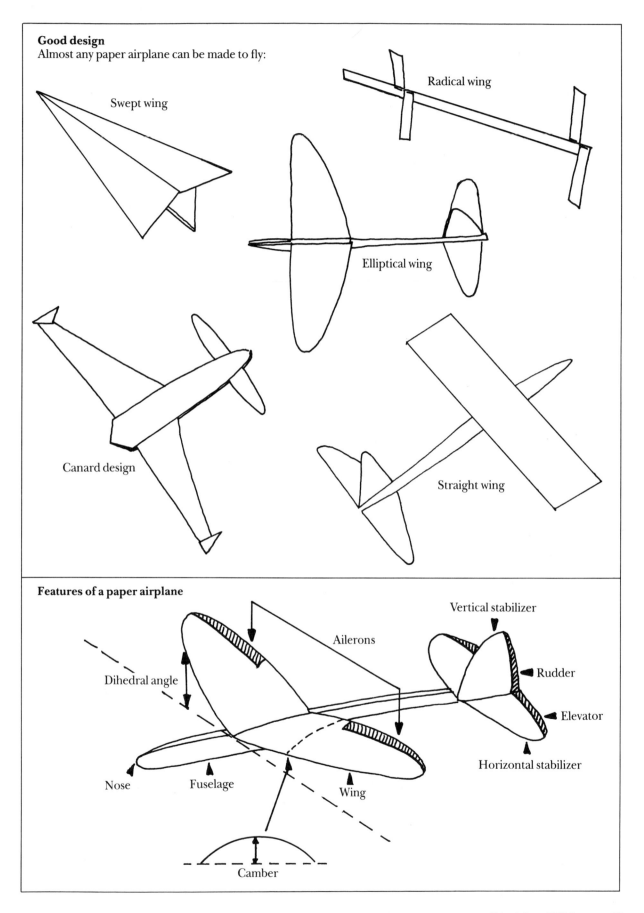

Swept wing

Radical wing

Elliptical wing

Canard design

Straight wing

Features of a paper airplane

Vertical stabilizer

Ailerons

Rudder

Dihedral angle

Elevator

Nose

Fuselage

Wing

Horizontal stabilizer

Camber

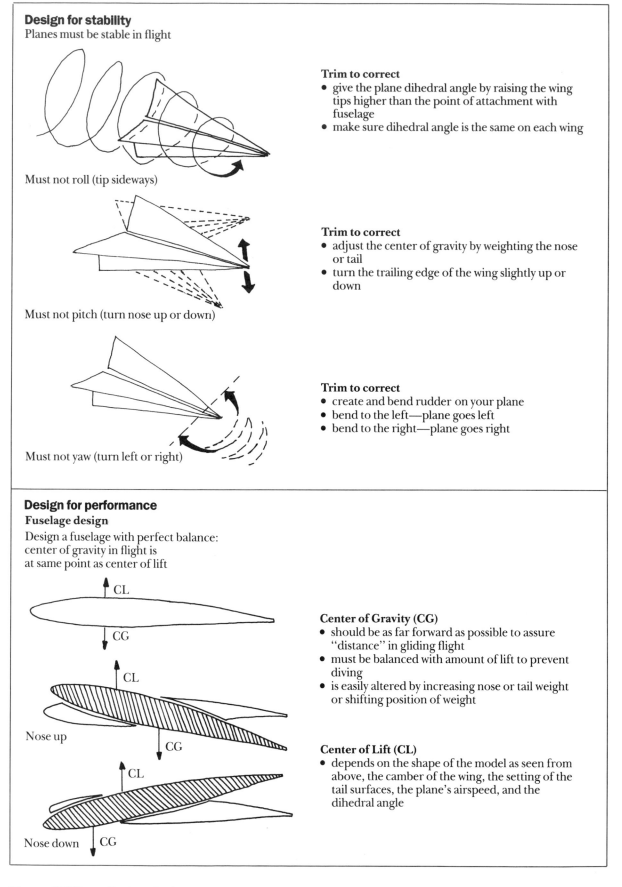

Design for stability
Planes must be stable in flight

Must not roll (tip sideways)

Trim to correct
- give the plane dihedral angle by raising the wing tips higher than the point of attachment with fuselage
- make sure dihedral angle is the same on each wing

Must not pitch (turn nose up or down)

Trim to correct
- adjust the center of gravity by weighting the nose or tail
- turn the trailing edge of the wing slightly up or down

Must not yaw (turn left or right)

Trim to correct
- create and bend rudder on your plane
- bend to the left—plane goes left
- bend to the right—plane goes right

Design for performance
Fuselage design
Design a fuselage with perfect balance: center of gravity in flight is at same point as center of lift

CL

CG

CL

Nose up

CG

CL

Nose down   CG

Center of Gravity (CG)
- should be as far forward as possible to assure "distance" in gliding flight
- must be balanced with amount of lift to prevent diving
- is easily altered by increasing nose or tail weight or shifting position of weight

Center of Lift (CL)
- depends on the shape of the model as seen from above, the camber of the wing, the setting of the tail surfaces, the plane's airspeed, and the dihedral angle

Wing design

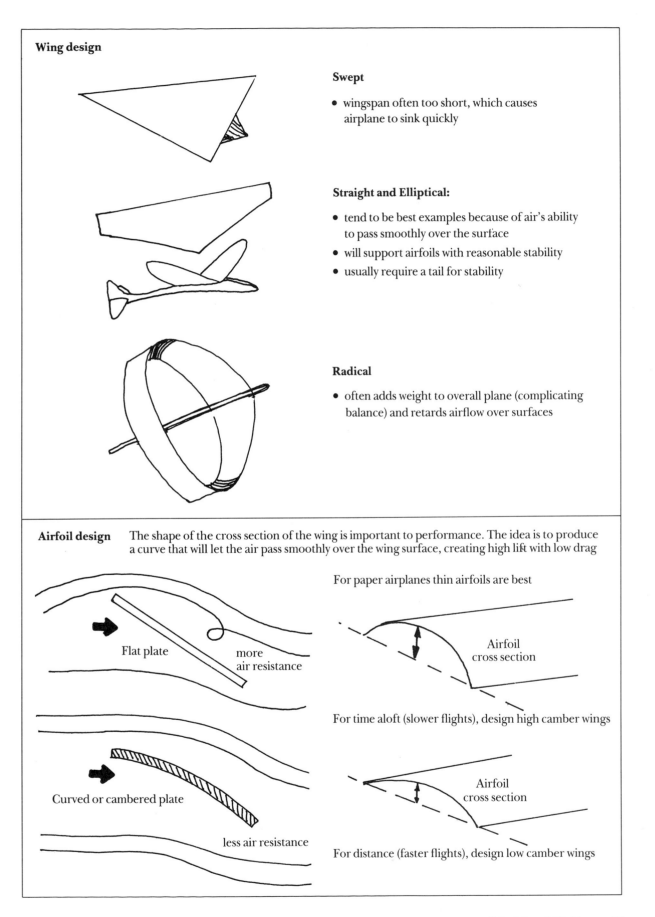

Swept

- wingspan often too short, which causes airplane to sink quickly

Straight and Elliptical:

- tend to be best examples because of air's ability to pass smoothly over the surface
- will support airfoils with reasonable stability
- usually require a tail for stability

Radical

- often adds weight to overall plane (complicating balance) and retards airflow over surfaces

Airfoil design The shape of the cross section of the wing is important to performance. The idea is to produce a curve that will let the air pass smoothly over the wing surface, creating high lift with low drag

Flat plate   more air resistance

Curved or cambered plate   less air resistance

For paper airplanes thin airfoils are best

Airfoil cross section

For time aloft (slower flights), design high camber wings

Airfoil cross section

For distance (faster flights), design low camber wings

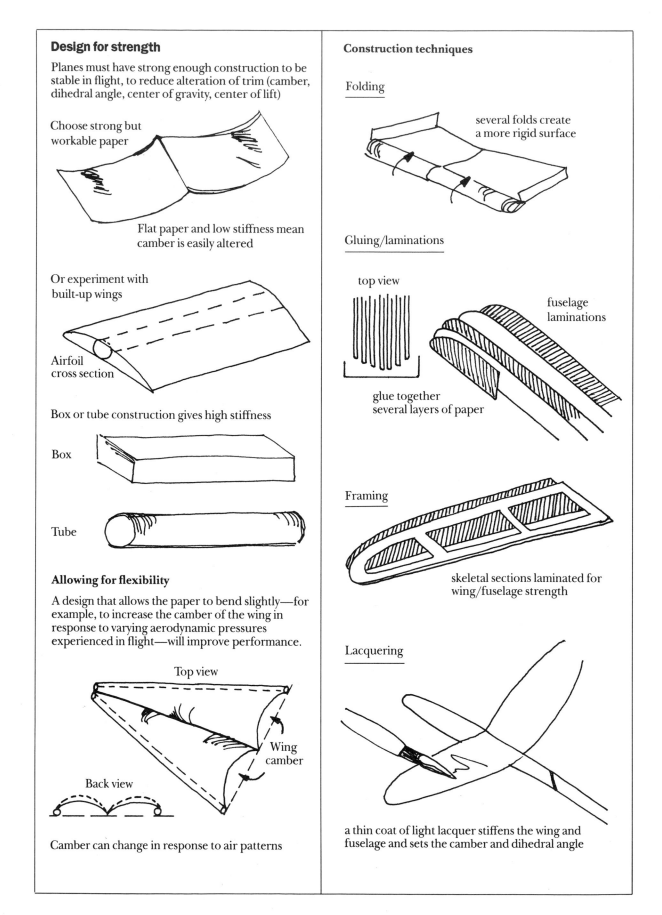

Design for strength

Planes must have strong enough construction to be stable in flight, to reduce alteration of trim (camber, dihedral angle, center of gravity, center of lift)

Choose strong but workable paper

Flat paper and low stiffness mean camber is easily altered

Or experiment with built-up wings

Airfoil cross section

Box or tube construction gives high stiffness

Box

Tube

Allowing for flexibility

A design that allows the paper to bend slightly—for example, to increase the camber of the wing in response to varying aerodynamic pressures experienced in flight—will improve performance.

Top view

Wing camber

Back view

Camber can change in response to air patterns

Construction techniques

Folding

several folds create a more rigid surface

Gluing/laminations

top view

fuselage laminations

glue together several layers of paper

Framing

skeletal sections laminated for wing/fuselage strength

Lacquering

a thin coat of light lacquer stiffens the wing and fuselage and sets the camber and dihedral angle

4.
PLANS
a do-it-yourself kit

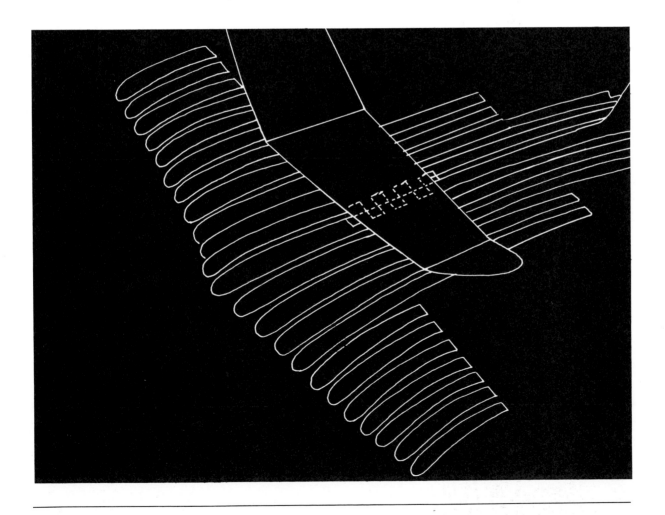

How To Use This Book

IN THIS SECTION you will find construction plans for eight paper airplanes. One was designed exclusively for this book by Dr. Y. Ninomiya; the others are winning designs from the Second Great International Paper Airplane Contest. Look them over carefully before beginning; some are much more difficult than others. Beginners may want to try Eltin Lucero's *Classic Schoolboy Dart*, Robert Meuser's *Paper Pussycat*, or Hironori Kurisu's *Rainbow* before attempting more advanced designs.

For each plane you will find illustrated instructions and numbered templates for each plane part. The templates are arranged so that you can cut them out of the book without damaging the instructions or part of another plane. Cut them out carefully and use them to trace the parts onto the paper from which you intend to build your plane. If you think you will build a design more than once, you might want to first trace the templates onto a heavier material; the cardboard that often comes with shirts from the cleaners makes excellent templates.

When you have chosen a design to build, read all the way through the instructions before you start working. You might also want to look carefully at the photographs of the plane in Chapter Two (all are pictured except Dr. Ninomiya's *Whitewings Racer*). Lay out the pattern parts carefully on your construction paper, filling a whole sheet of paper before you start cutting. This is particularly important when you use the Whitewings paper included with this book: there is enough Whitewings paper to build any of the designs included here, but only if you lay out the patterns so as not to waste it.

One further caution on laying out the parts to your plane: for maximum performance, use the correct orientation of your construction paper. A sheet of paper is more resistant to bending in one direction than in another. You can determine the bend-resistant orientation for any paper with the following procedure: Cut out a small square piece (about $2'' \times 2''$). Hold it with thumb and index finger on opposite edges and bend gently; then repeat with the other two edges. You will be able to feel the difference. Align your parts lengthwise along the direction that is most bend-resistant. For the Whitewings paper bound into this book, the bend-resistant direction should be vertically (along the length).

Whitewings paper

Whitewings paper was developed specifically for paper airplane construction. It is lightweight, extremely uniform, and yet unusually stiff, which gives it the remarkable property of holding the shape it is bent to and makes it much easier to construct and trim a plane.

Most ordinary paper is not stiff enough to hold a shape and has fibers aligned so that it has a lot of bend-resistance in one direction and very little in the other, which is not good for paper airplane construction. Whitewings paper is made by a very expensive manufacturing process designed to give it more uniform properties; its bend-resistance is much closer, but still not identical, in both directions. The paper is included in Whitewings paper airplane kits, but cannot be purchased separately, so use your three sheets (bound inside the back cover of this book) carefully.

Materials

For high-performance airplanes, the quality of the construction paper is important. For most designs, ordinary typing, copier, or notebook paper is not very good, although you may want to try a design first with whatever paper you have, just to get experience in building it. If you want to save your Whitewings paper (or when you run out of it), try to get sheets of index card stock or Japanese Kent paper at your stationery store. The bristol board available at most art stores is heavier but workable; you want the kind with a smooth finish (called plate bristol board), not vellum. Another reasonably good material is cover stock, such as is used for printing magazine covers. You can find it at some printer's supply stores or good stationery stores (the 60-pound or 70-pound weight is best), or simply recycle old magazine covers. If none of these is available, your best choice is probably a good bond typing paper, although it may be too flexible for some designs unless you laminate two sheets together.

Glues and Lacquers

Japanese master airplane builders use Cemedine C glue. For a reasonably close U.S. equivalent, we suggest Itoya-O-Glue or Pentel Roll, light transparent glues available at many stationery stores. If these are not available, Elmer's glue (the white paper glue) is a good choice; dilute it slightly with water. You may want to experiment with other glues as well. Some designs included in this chapter call for specific additional glues.

To help set the shape of your plane when it is done and protect it from damage during handling, you may want to apply a thin coat of lacquer or varnish. A water-soluble lacquer dries fastest. Don't use too much.

Tools

Razor blades or X-acto blades (which are safer) can be used to cut out your airplane parts if you have a very steady hand. Otherwise a good sharp pair of scissors is the best tool. A ruler or straightedge will be useful too. Where a design calls for scoring the paper, a pointed but blunt object such as a knitting needle is best. Some designs call for tape as well as glue; ordinary transparent tape is best. Tape can also be useful to secure corners against landing impact, but don't use too much, because it adds weight.

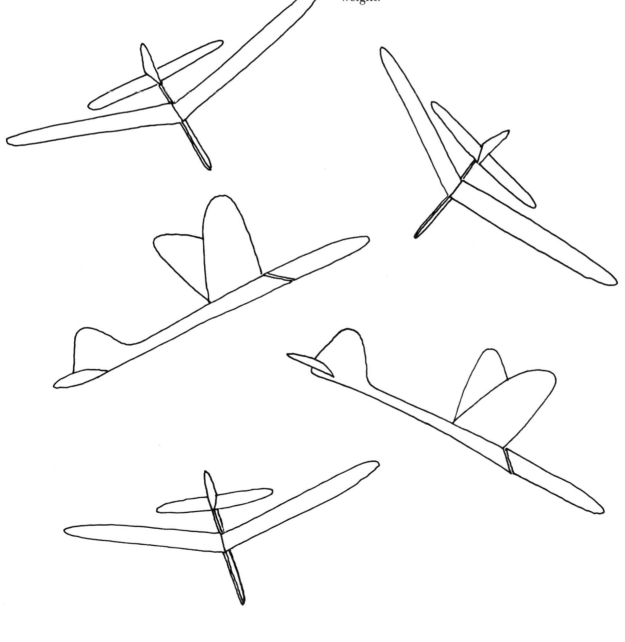

Dr. Y. Ninomiya's Test Flying and Trimming Tips

CAREFUL DESIGN and construction of your paper airplane is very important, as explained in Chapter Three of this book. But these are not the only factors determining how a plane performs. To fly its best, every paper airplane needs to be carefully trimmed. Here are some of the basics of trimming as taught by Japanese master Dr. Y. Ninomiya. These will apply to most paper airplanes.

Test Flight

Try to test fly your plane when there is no wind or only a very light one. Throw your plane straight into the wind. When test flying your plane indoors, always try to throw it toward a curtain. Don't throw it upward, but toss it gently forward, aiming it horizontally or slightly downward. The goal is a test flight that is straight and smooth.

Observe your plane's performance. See whether it flies to the left or the right, or whether it noses up (stalling) or noses down abruptly (diving). If so, your plane needs trimming to correct these faults.

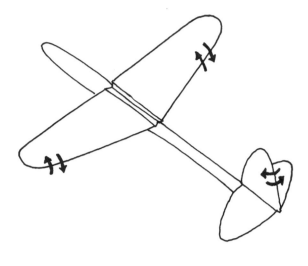

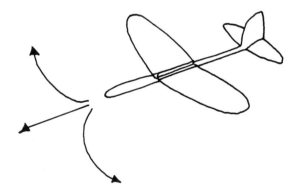

Plane curves to the right:

Bend the right aileron (the trailing edge of the right wing tip) slightly lower; or

Bend the rudder (the rear edge of the vertical stabilizer) slightly to the left; or

Bend the left aileron (the trailing edge of the left wing tip) slightly upwards.

Note: Trimming changes are minor adjustments (1° - 2°). It is not necessary to make cuts in the wings; just bend the appropriate areas slightly with your fingers to adjust the ailerons and rudder.

Plane curves to the left:

Lower the left aileron (bend the trailing edge of the left wing tip slightly downwards); or

Bend the rudder (the rear edge of the vertical stabilizer) slightly to the right; or

Raise the right aileron (bend the trailing edge of the right wing tip slightly upwards).

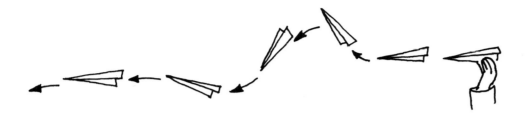

Plane noses up (losing speed and stalling):

Bend the elevators (the trailing edges of the horizontal stabilizer) slightly down. The plane will fly faster and the nose of the plane will stay down better, resisting stalling.

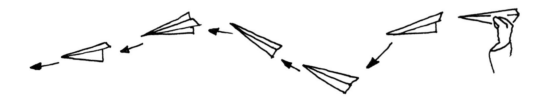

Plane noses down (suddenly gaining speed and diving):

Bend the elevators (the trailing edges of the horizontal stabilizer) slightly upward. The nose of the plane will point up better, resisting diving.

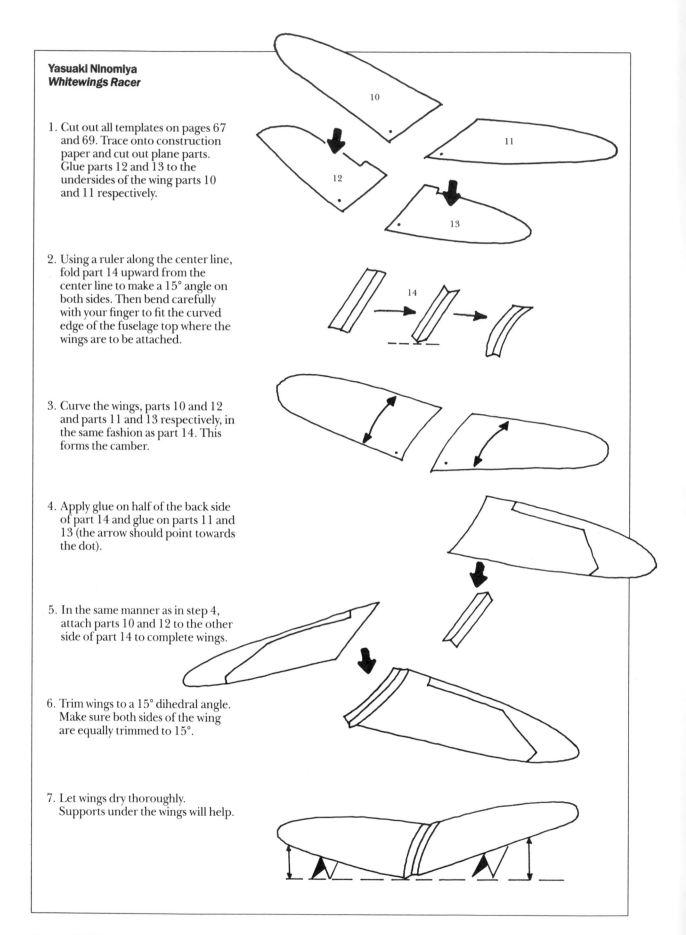

Yasuaki Ninomiya
Whitewings Racer

1. Cut out all templates on pages 67 and 69. Trace onto construction paper and cut out plane parts. Glue parts 12 and 13 to the undersides of the wing parts 10 and 11 respectively.

2. Using a ruler along the center line, fold part 14 upward from the center line to make a 15° angle on both sides. Then bend carefully with your finger to fit the curved edge of the fuselage top where the wings are to be attached.

3. Curve the wings, parts 10 and 12 and parts 11 and 13 respectively, in the same fashion as part 14. This forms the camber.

4. Apply glue on half of the back side of part 14 and glue on parts 11 and 13 (the arrow should point towards the dot).

5. In the same manner as in step 4, attach parts 10 and 12 to the other side of part 14 to complete wings.

6. Trim wings to a 15° dihedral angle. Make sure both sides of the wing are equally trimmed to 15°.

7. Let wings dry thoroughly. Supports under the wings will help.

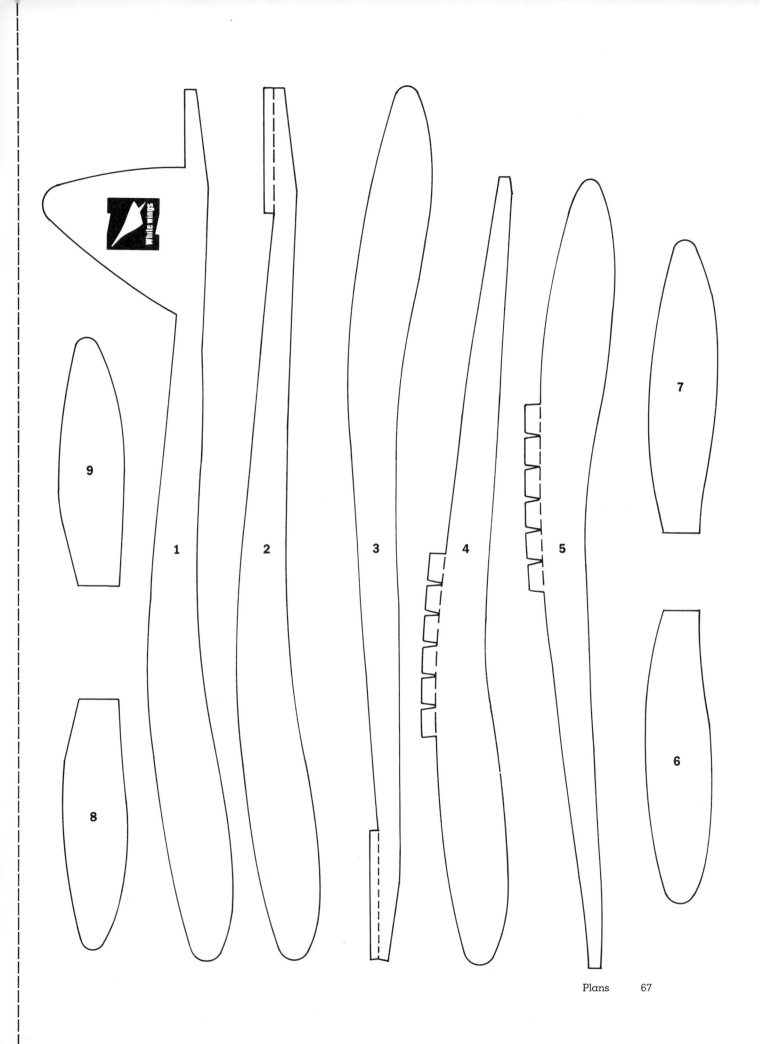

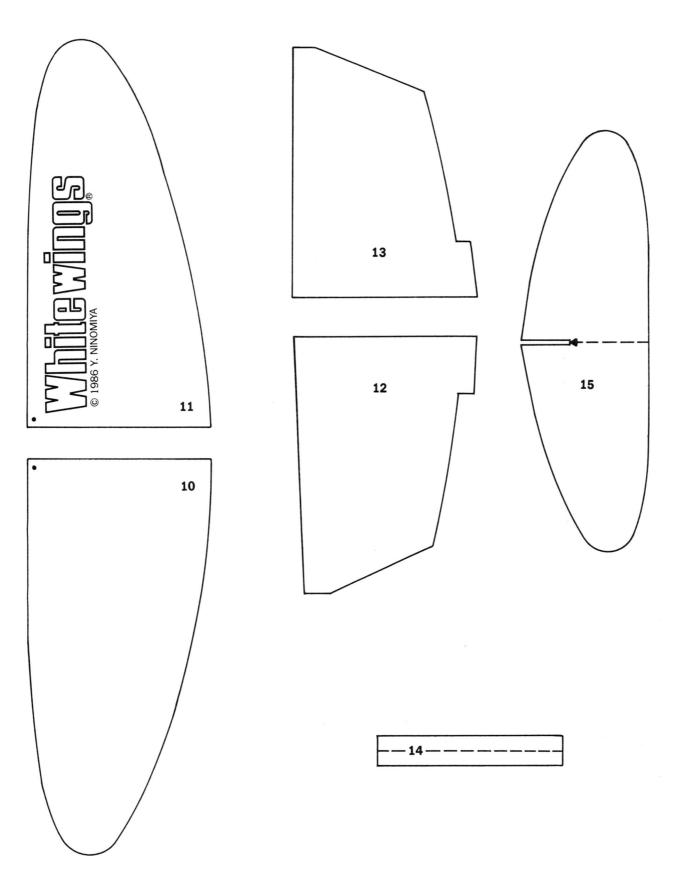

11

Whitewings®

© 1986 Y. NINOMIYA

10

13

12

15

14

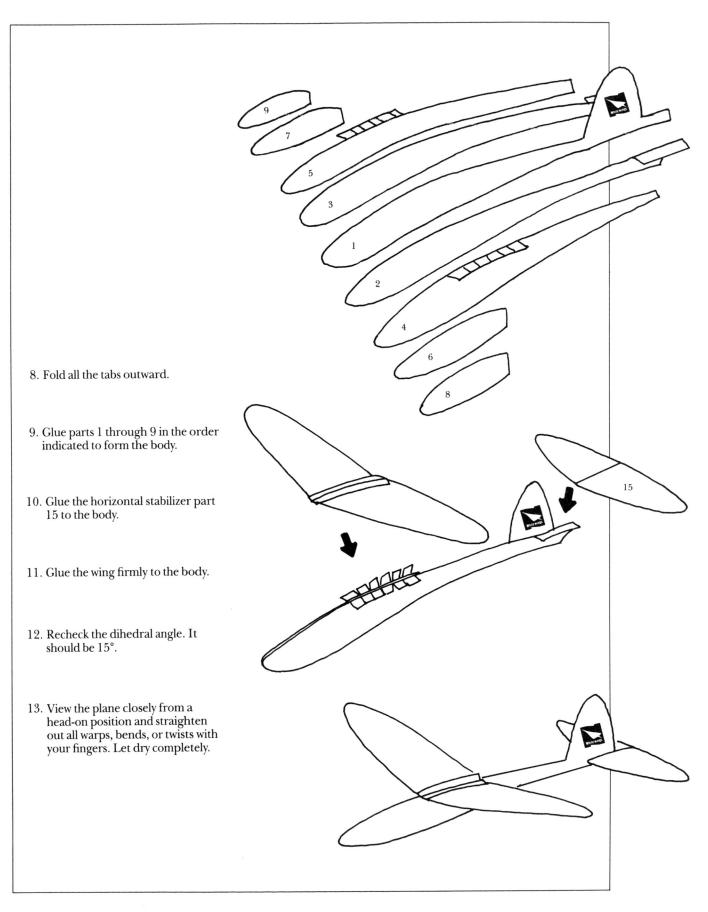

8. Fold all the tabs outward.

9. Glue parts 1 through 9 in the order indicated to form the body.

10. Glue the horizontal stabilizer part 15 to the body.

11. Glue the wing firmly to the body.

12. Recheck the dihedral angle. It should be 15°.

13. View the plane closely from a head-on position and straighten out all warps, bends, or twists with your fingers. Let dry completely.

Akio Kobayashi
Distance/Professional

Fuselage

1. Cut out part l. Bend every other tab outward. Cut out part 2 (2 pieces). Glue one on each side of part 1. This is the core of the fuselage.

2. Cut out part 3 (2 pieces). Glue one on each side of the fuselage.

3. Cut out part 4 (4 pieces). Glue two on each side of the fuselage.

4. Cut out part 5 (14 pieces). Glue seven pieces on each side of the fuselage.

Wing

5. Cut out the wing section, part 7. Work camber into it so that the curvature of the wing matches the shape of the fuselage. Bend the wing at the center to match the dihedral angle guide shown in the illustration. Carefully turn the tips of the wing upward as shown in the the illustration. Carefully glue the wing on to the fuselage tabs, making sure the dihedral angle on each side is the same.

Horizontal Stabilizer

6. Cut out the horizontal stabilizer, part 6. Work some camber (concave downward) into the part. This will assist the main wing in lifting the plane. Glue the horizontal stabilizer onto the fuselage as indicated.

7. Carefully apply a thin coat of clear lacquer all over the plane to hold the camber and to help keep moisture off the paper.

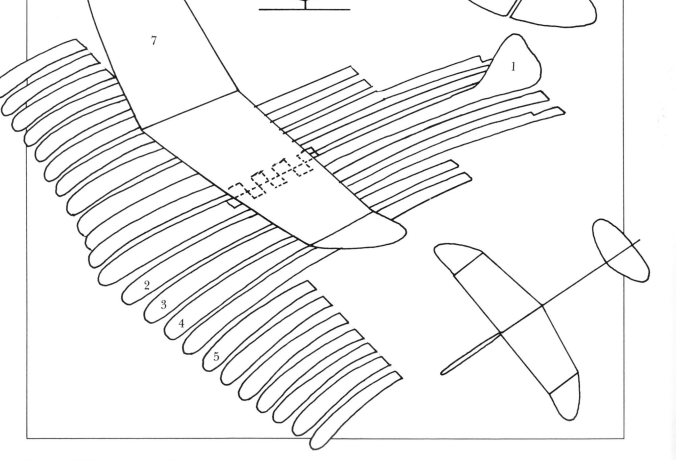

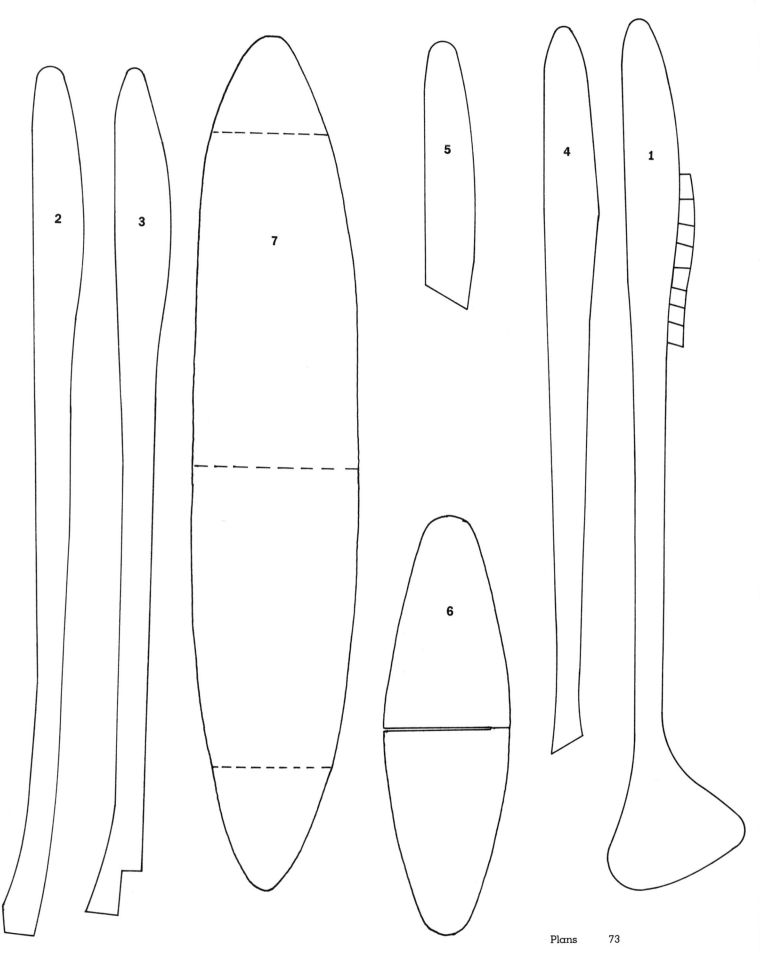

Robert Meuser
Paper Pussycat
Distance/Non-professional

1. Cut out three 13½″ × 1″ fuselage pieces. Fold each piece in half
   (½″ thickness) and score slightly (do not cut through) with a razor blade
   to facilitate fold. Crease on cut line.

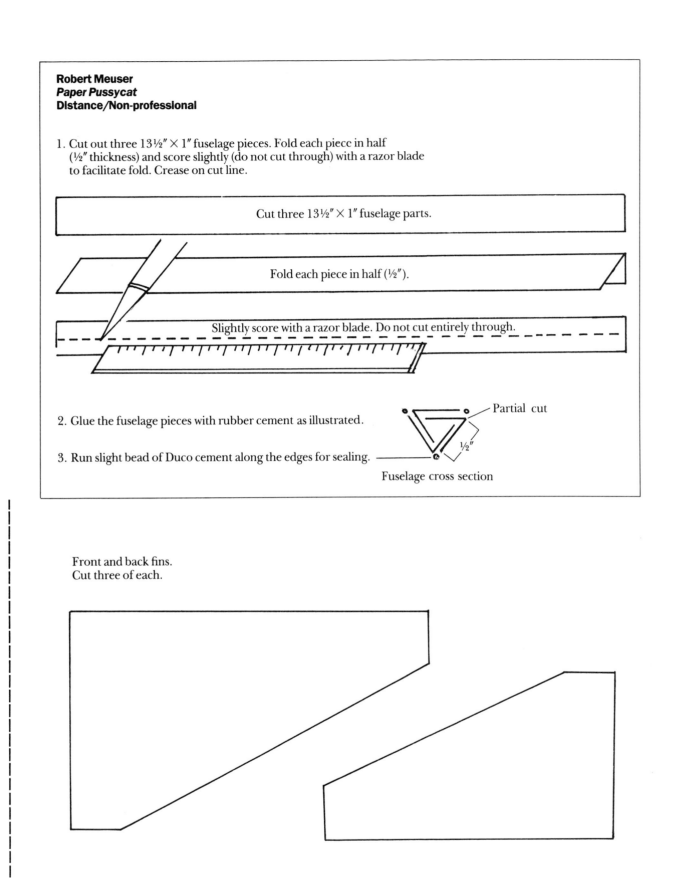

Cut three 13½″ × 1″ fuselage parts.

Fold each piece in half (½″).

Slightly score with a razor blade. Do not cut entirely through.

2. Glue the fuselage pieces with rubber cement as illustrated.

Partial cut

3. Run slight bead of Duco cement along the edges for sealing.

½″

Fuselage cross section

Front and back fins.
Cut three of each.

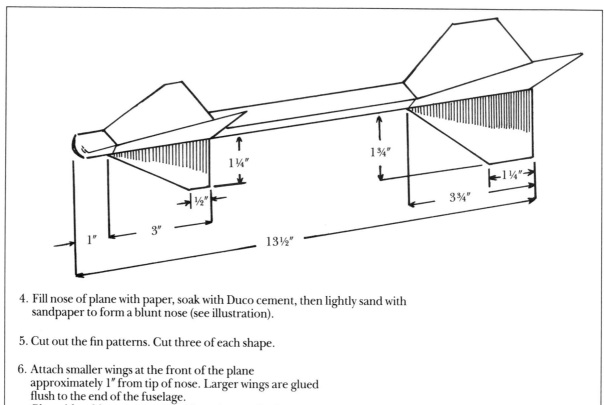

4. Fill nose of plane with paper, soak with Duco cement, then lightly sand with sandpaper to form a blunt nose (see illustration).

5. Cut out the fin patterns. Cut three of each shape.

6. Attach smaller wings at the front of the plane
approximately 1″ from tip of nose. Larger wings are glued
flush to the end of the fuselage.
Glue with rubber cement, attaching wings to the flat sides of the fuselage.

Eltin Lucero
Classic Schoolboy Dart
Distance/Junior

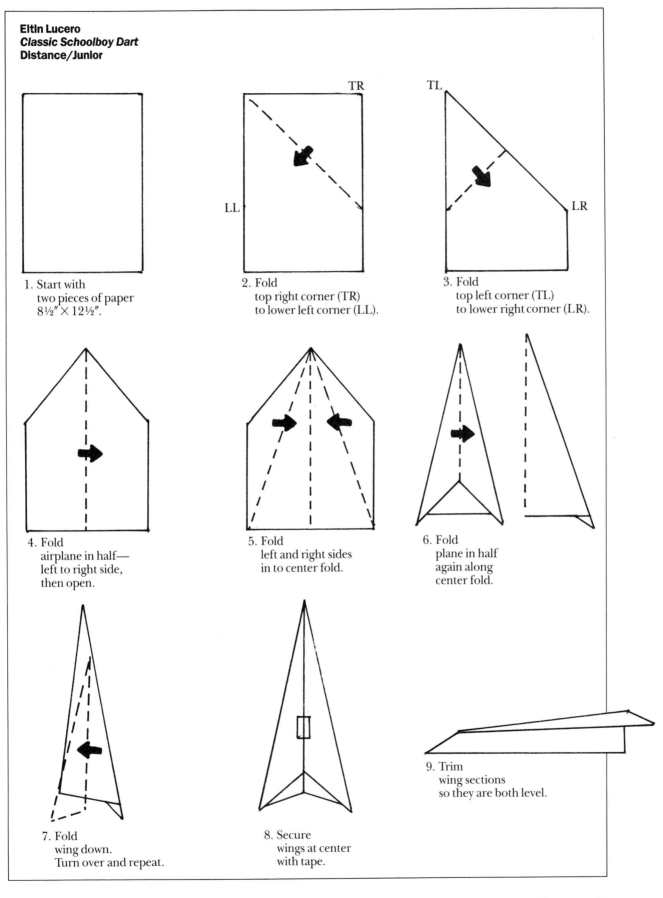

1. Start with
   two pieces of paper
   8½″ × 12½″.

2. Fold
   top right corner (TR)
   to lower left corner (LL).

3. Fold
   top left corner (TL)
   to lower right corner (LR).

4. Fold
   airplane in half—
   left to right side,
   then open.

5. Fold
   left and right sides
   in to center fold.

6. Fold
   plane in half
   again along
   center fold.

7. Fold
   wing down.
   Turn over and repeat.

8. Secure
   wings at center
   with tape.

9. Trim
   wing sections
   so they are both level.

Tatuo Yoshida
Asuka
Time Aloft/Professional

Fuselage

The fuselage is made up of a number of stiff paper cut-outs laminated to form the shape desired.

1. Cut out the following fuselage parts.

Part	Quantity
1	1
2	2
3	4
4	2
5	2
6	2

Follow the assembly drawing for the location of each part.

2. Glue a part 2 on each side of part l.

3. Glue two of part 3 to each side of the assembly (next to part 2).

4. Glue a part 4 to each side of the assembly (next to part 3).

5. Glue a part 5 to each side of the assembly (next to part 4), gluing them on the nose as shown in the illustration.

6. Glue a part 6 to each side of the assembly (next to part 5) by gluing them on the nose as shown in the illustration.

Stabilizer

7. Cut out part l0 and glue to the rear bottom of the fuselage assembly. The most curved portion is the forward part of the stabilizer.

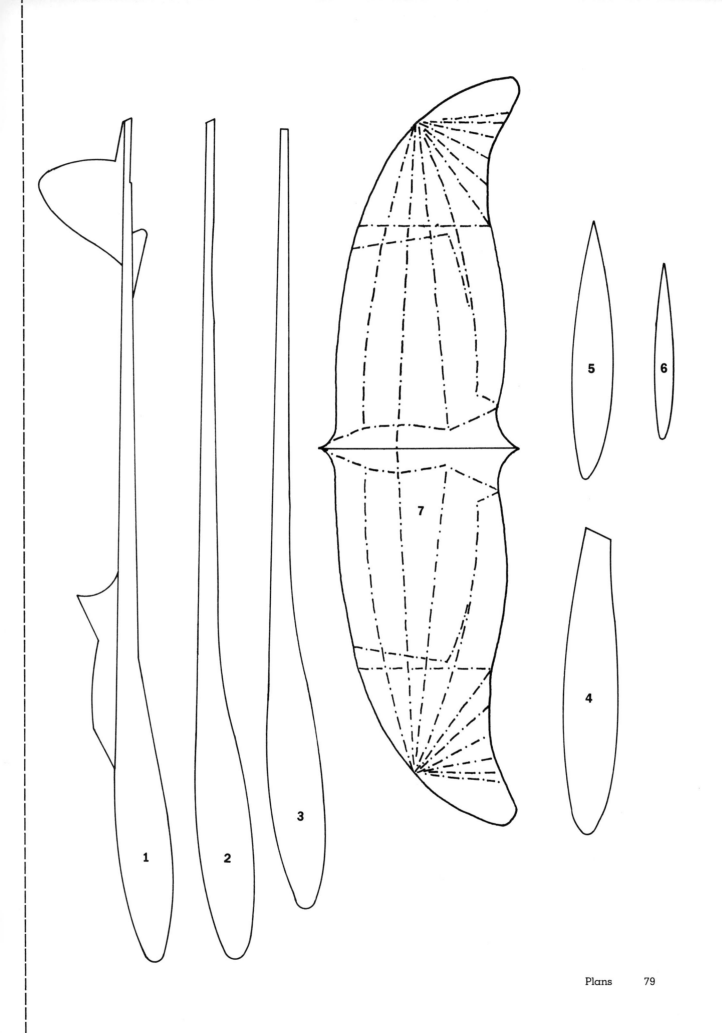

Wing

8. Cut out the following parts:

Part	Quantity
7	1
8	1
9	2

9. Glue part 8 to part 7. The side of the wing containing part 8 is the underside.

10. Glue parts 9 to the underside of the wing assembly (next to part 8). Locate the two 9 pieces at the center of the wing with a gap at the center as wide as the body width of the top of the fuselage where the wing will be placed.

11. Score the upper surface of the wing at the center and along the dot-dash line near the wing tips. You should use a blunt, rounded instrument such as a knitting needle; it should make an impression in the paper, but not cut or mark it.

12. Warp some camber (concave down) into the wing surface. Bend a dihedral angle of about 10°-15° into the wing at the center. Bend an additional 10°-15° into each wing tip at the outer score marks. Make sure that the wing tip dihedrals are symmetrical.

13. Glue the wing assembly to the top of the fuselage at the point shown on the main fuselage. Fit the wing on the top of the fuselage tab. Glue securely. Be sure that the dihedral angle is symmetrical with respect to the fuselage.

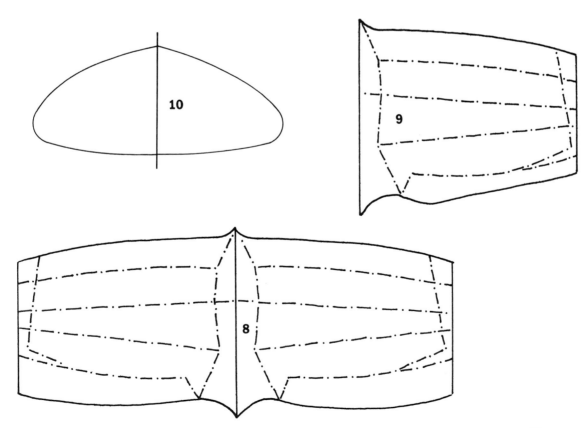

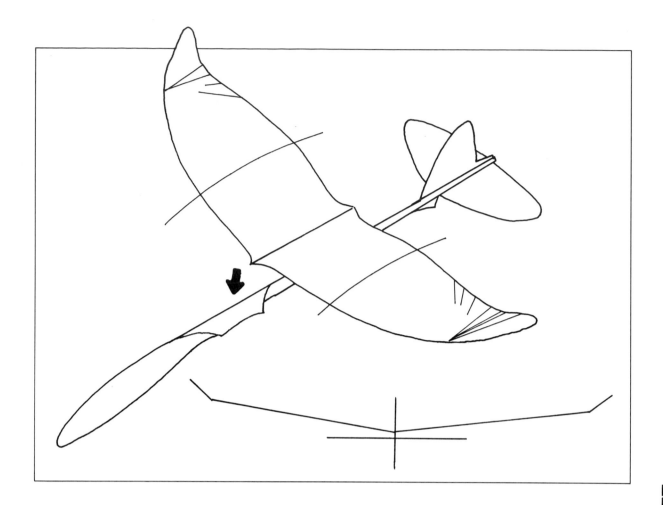

Yoshiharu Ishii
Time Aloft/Non–professional

Fuselage

1. Cut out parts 1, 2, and 3. (Cut one extra of part 1, label it 1A, and set it aside to use later as a pattern for Step 6.)

2. Cut out the three areas marked "c" on the fuselage pieces above. Glue parts 2 and 3 to each side of part 1 to form the core of the fuselage.

3. Cut out parts 4, 6, 8, 10 and 12 and glue them on one side of the fuselage in the order mentioned. Then cut out parts 5, 7, 9, 11 and 13 and glue on the other side of the fuselage in the same manner. **Do not glue the tabs together at the midpoint and at the tail end of parts 4 and 5.**

Wing

4. Cut out part 14, including the sections marked "d," and part 15. **Do not cut the heavy marked lines at the center of parts 14 and 15.** Glue part 14 to part 15.

5. When the gluing of part 14 is dry, make cuts as indicated on the heavy marked lines at the center of the wing.

6. The bottomside of the wing is the side that contains part 14. Warp a camber into the wing with the concave portion on the bottom. Curvature of camber should be adjusted so that it closely matches the curvature of part 1A with maximum depth at about one third of the distance back from the front (from the leading edge).

7. Cut out part 16 and make a slight fold along the dotted line. Bend a dihedral in the wing of about 10°-15°.

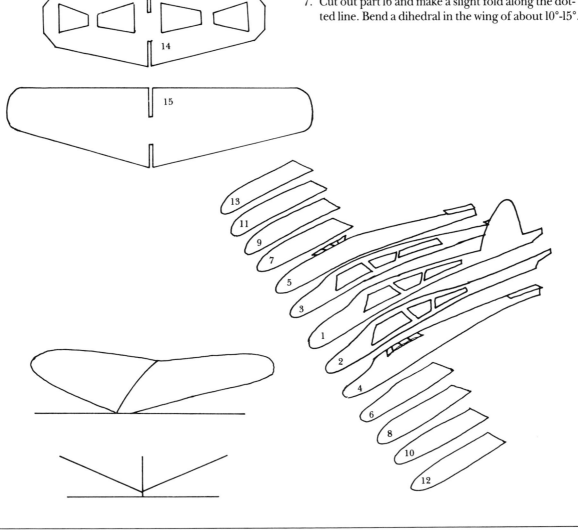

8. Fold the tabs near the midpoint of parts 4 and 5 outwards so they form a bed for the wing to sit on. Glue the wing onto this bed with the front towards the front of the fuselage. When the glue is dry adjust the fold in part 16 to be about the same angle as the wing dihedral. Glue part 16 on top of the center of the wing (next to part 15) to stiffen the dihedral setting. Be sure the wing is not tilted with respect to the fuselage.

9. Cut out the horizontal stabilizer, part 17. Fold the tabs at the ends of parts 4 and 5 outwards to form a platform for the horizontal stabilizer. Glue the horizontal stabilizer to this platform with the front pointing forward. Be sure that the stabilizer is at right angles to the fuselage.

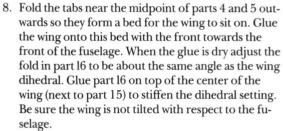

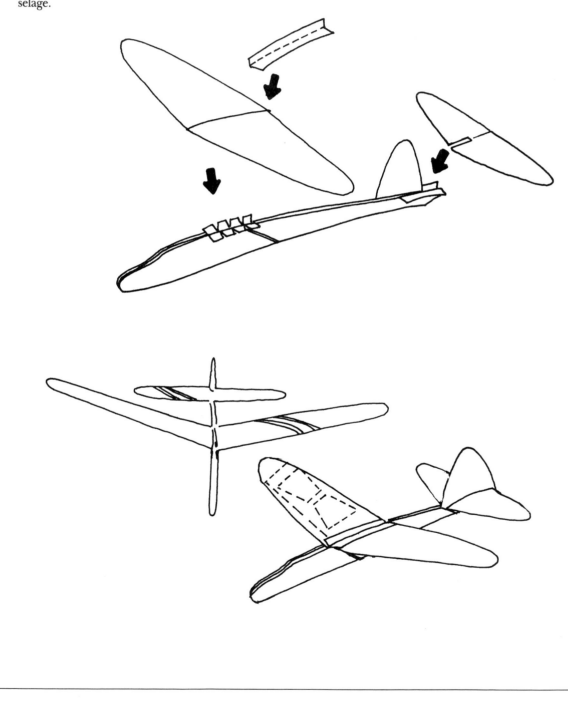

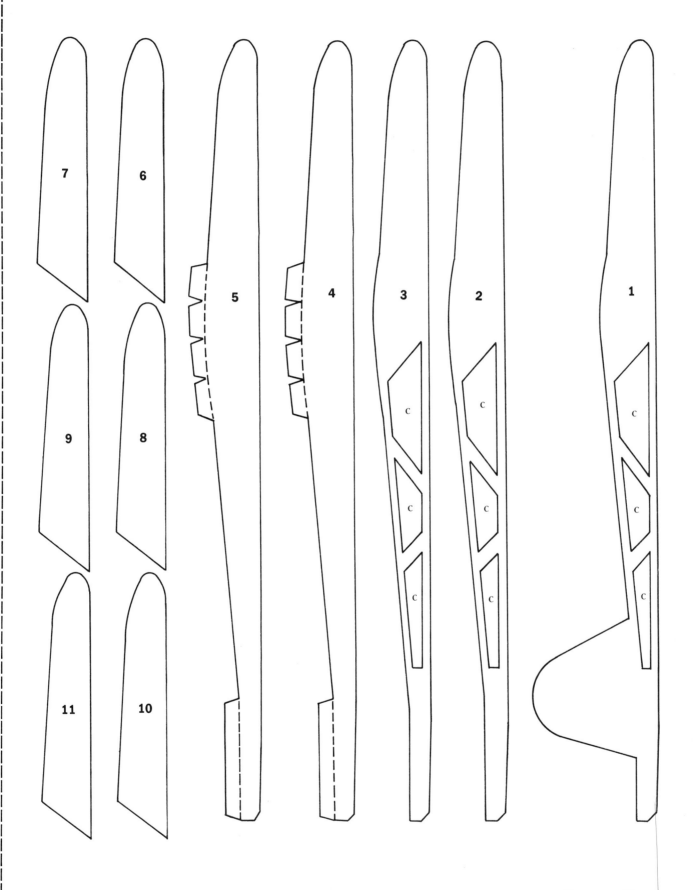

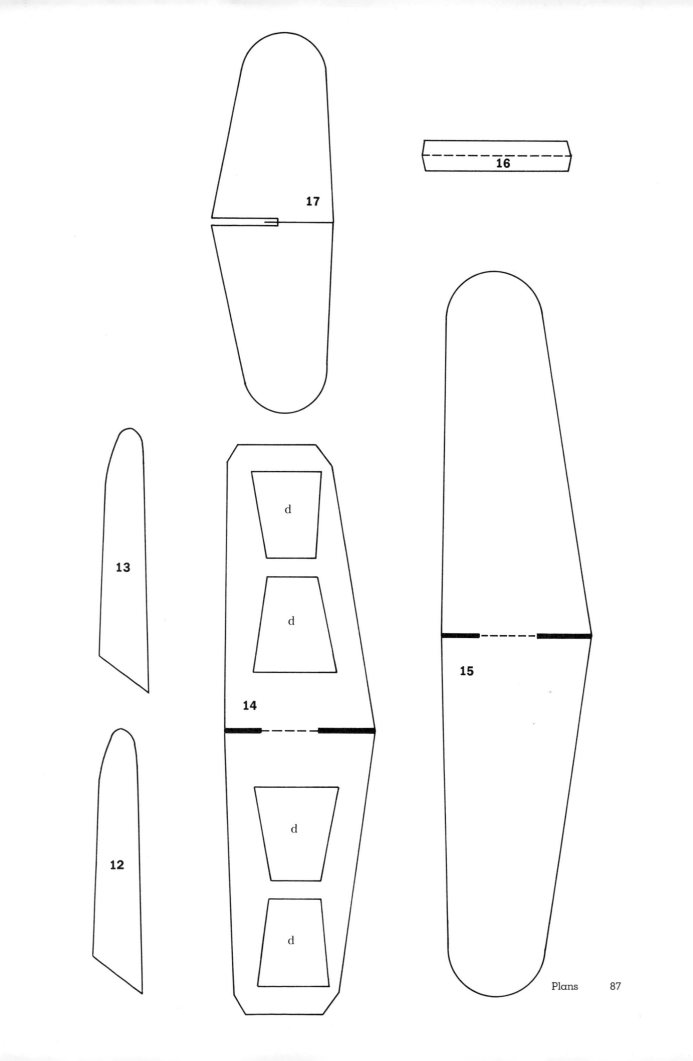

Hironori Kurisu
Rainbow
Time Aloft/Junior

This is an easy paper airplane design to begin your orientation to paper laminate design.

Fuselage

1. Cut out parts 1, 2, 3, and 4. Score the dash lines at the tail end of parts 3 and 4. You should use a blunt, rounded instrument such as a knitting needle; it should make an impression in the paper, but not cut or mark it. Fold the tabs at the tail ends of parts 3 and 4 along the score lines. Be sure that the tabs fold in opposite directions.

2. Glue parts 1 and 2 together.

3. Glue parts 3 and 4 to the fuselage assembly, one on each side. Be sure that the folded tabs at the rear end of the fuselage point outwards.

4. Cut out parts 5 and 6. Score the dash lines along the tops of these parts. Fold the tabs outward along the score lines. Glue parts 5 and 6 to the fuselage assembly with the tabs pointing outwards.

5. Cut out parts 7 and 8. Glue on to each side of the fuselage at the nose.

6. Cut out two each of parts 9 and 10. Glue both parts 9 to one side of the fuselage nose and both parts 10 to the other side.

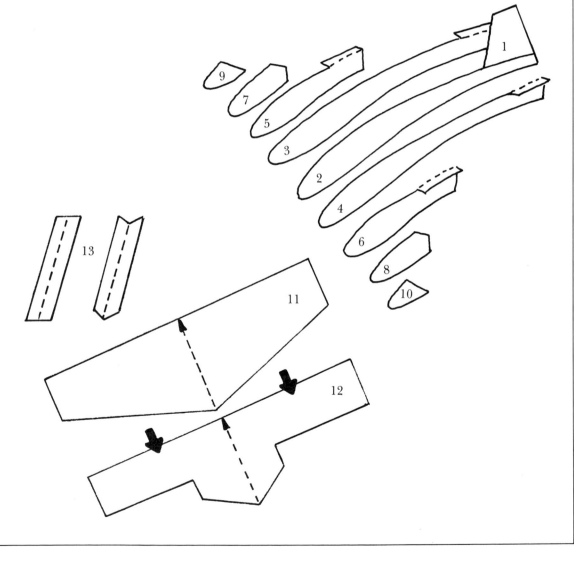

Wing

7. Cut out parts ll, 12, and 13. Glue part ll to part 12. The side of the wing with part 12 is the bottom of the wing.

8. Score the wing from leading edge to trailing edge at the center. Warp a small amount of camber into the wing so that it fits smoothly onto the tabs near the middle of the fuselage. Bend about 10-15° of dihedral angle into the wing along the score marks.

9. Score part l3 along the dash center mark. Bend part l3 along the score mark until its angle is such that it is about the same as the wing dihedral angle.

10. Glue the wing onto the tabs on the top of the fuselage. The leading edge of the wing, which is the straight edge, should be flush with the front tabs. Glue part l3 onto the center of the top of the wing to strengthen the center joint. Be sure that the wing is square with the fuselage.

Stabilizer

11. Cut out part l4. Carefully cut down the stabilizer middle as indicated. Glue part l4 to the tabs on the bottom of the fuselage at the rear end. The straight edge should be flush with the end of the fuselage. Be sure that the stabilizer is square with the fuselage.

12. Recheck the dihedral angle in the wings.

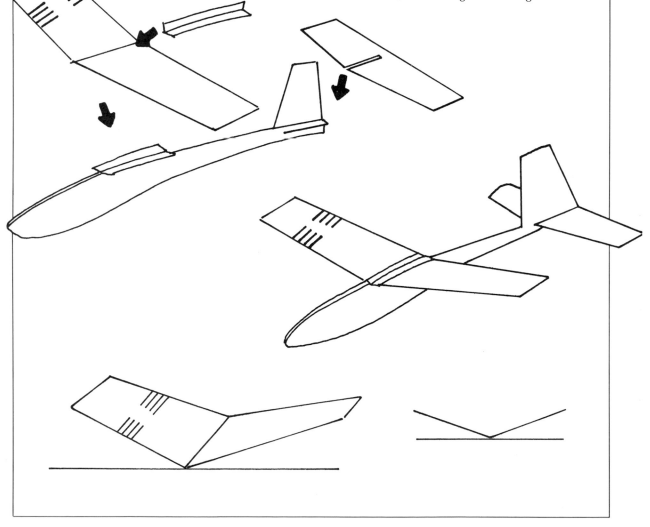

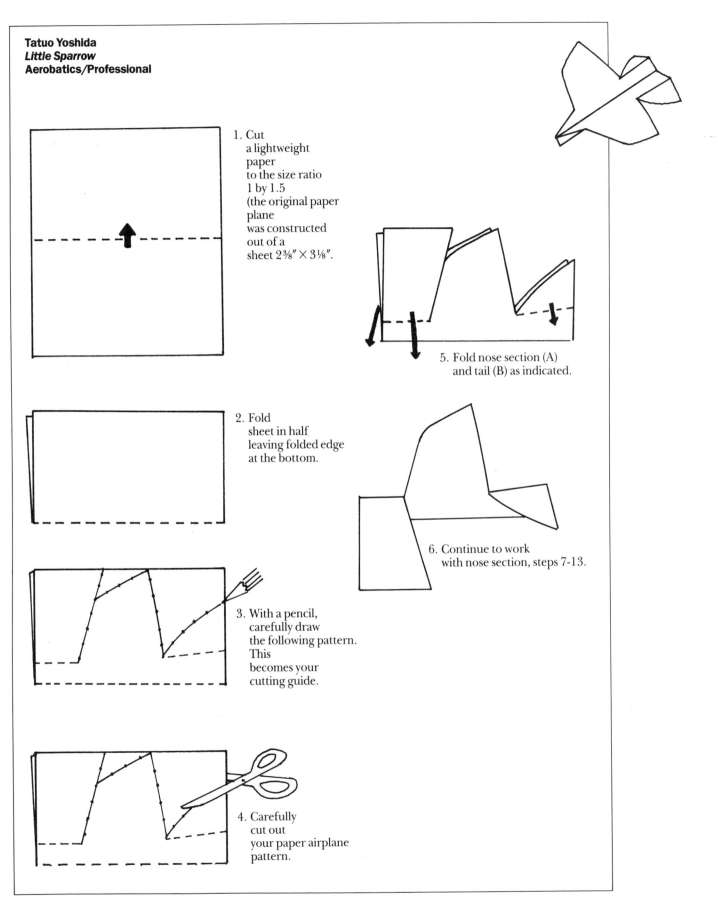

1. Cut
   a lightweight
   paper
   to the size ratio
   1 by 1.5
   (the original paper
   plane
   was constructed
   out of a
   sheet 2⅜″ × 3⅛″.

2. Fold
   sheet in half
   leaving folded edge
   at the bottom.

3. With a pencil,
   carefully draw
   the following pattern.
   This
   becomes your
   cutting guide.

4. Carefully
   cut out
   your paper airplane
   pattern.

5. Fold nose section (A)
   and tail (B) as indicated.

6. Continue to work
   with nose section, steps 7-13.

7. Fold top tip down.

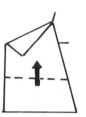
8. Fold top down.

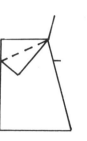
9. Fold bottom half up.

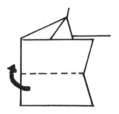
10. Repeat on other side.

11. Fold bottom flap up.

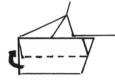
12. Repeat on other side.

13. With tape, secure last fold.

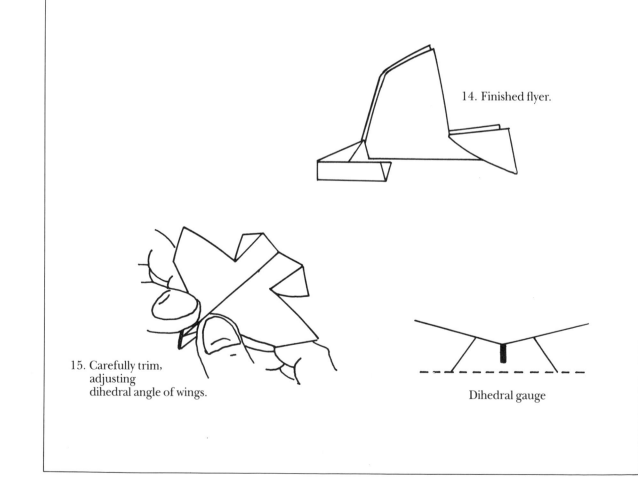
14. Finished flyer.

15. Carefully trim, adjusting dihedral angle of wings.

Dihedral gauge

5.

RESOURCES

AERODYNAMICS—The study of the properties of air in motion and how it affects bodies moving through it.

AILERON—a horizontal control surface at the trailing edge of a wing, or part of the trailing edge of the wing itself; ailerons are raised or lowered (or bent up or down) to alter the flow of air over the wing and hence induce or prevent rolling.

ALTITUDE—The height of an airplane above sea level; sometimes, the height above the ground.

ATTACK, ANGLE OF—The amount an airplane's wings are slanted against the airflow; the angle between the direction the plane is headed and a line drawn from the leading edge to the trailing edge of the wing.

ATTITUDE—How an airplane is pointed relative to the ground or to its flight path—level, nose up, nose down, etc.

BANK—To dip during a turn by raising the outside wing.

CAMBER—The curvature of a wing from leading to trailing edge.

CANARD—A type of aircraft in which the wings are located near the rear of the plane with the horizontal stabilizers in front.

CENTER OF GRAVITY—The balance point of a plane; the point through which gravity appears to act.

CENTER OF LIFT—The point at which the lift seems to be exerted when the plane is flying.

CONTROL SURFACES—Surfaces that can be bent or moved to control airflow and hence the operation of a plane; ailerons, elevators, elevons, rudders.

DIHEDRAL ANGLE—The amount by which the wings are slanted above the horizontal; the angle between the wing and the horizontal at the point where the wings join the fuselage.

DRAG—The force or resistance exerted by the air on a body moving through it.

ELEVATOR—a horizontal control surface at the trailing edge of the horizontal stabilizers that can be raised or lowered (or bent up or down) to alter airflow and hence induce or control pitching.

ELEVON—a control surface that acts as a combined aileron and elevator.

FIN—A vertical fore-and-aft surface extending above the other parts of the model; fins help provide directional stability.

FUSELAGE—the body of a plane.

GLIDE ANGLE—The slope of a glider's flight path, measured from the horizontal; also, the ratio of lift to drag. The less altitude lost when gliding a given horizontal distance, the smaller the glide angle and the better the glider.

GLIDER—A heavier-than-air, engineless aircraft that flies by gliding, such as a paper airplane.

LAMINATION—Gluing several layers of material together to obtain a stronger or stiffer structure.

LEADING EDGE—The forward edge of the wing or horizontal stabilizer.

LIFT—The force generated by the flow of air around a wing that allows an airplane to fly; the amount of force acting upward against the wings of a plane.

MANEUVER—to fly other than in straight, level flight; to turn, climb, dive, or execute some other flight pattern.

NOSE HEAVY—A condition in which the center of gravity is located more to the front of the plane than the center of lift, with the result that the plane tends to dive.

PITCH—To nose up or nose down.

ROLL—To raise one wing tip while lowering the other; to rotate the plane about its longitudinal axis.

RUDDER—A vertical control surface at the trailing edge of the vertical stabilizer or tail that can be moved right or left to alter the flow of air and hence initiate or control yawing.

STALL—Abrupt loss of lift occurring when the plane noses up too high or the wings have too high an angle of attack.

TEMPLATE—a pattern or guide to cutting out a part.

TRAILING EDGE—The rear edge of a wing or horizontal stabilizer.

TRIM—To make minor adjustments to control surfaces of a paper airplane to correct a tendency to pitch, roll, or yaw.

VERTICAL STABILIZER—a vertical surface usually at the rear of an airplane that aids directional and lateral stability; a tail.

WING—The portion of an airplane or glider that generates lift.

WINGSPAN—The distance from wing tip to wing tip.

YAW—To turn to the right or left.

Contest Records

1967 Contest

Time Aloft
First Professional	Frederick Hooven	10.2 seconds
First Non-professional	Jerry Brinkman	9.9 seconds

Distance
First Professional	Louis Schultz	58'2"
First Non-professional	Robert Meuser	91'6"

1985 Contest

Time Aloft
First Professional	Tatuo Yoshida	16.06 seconds
First Non-professional	Yoshiharu Ishii	9.80 seconds

Distance
First Professional	Akio Kobayashi	122'8"
First Non-professional	Robert Meuser	141'4"

Guinness Book of World Records

Indoor Distance	Tony Felch LaCrosse, WI 5/21/85	193'
Indoor Time Aloft (12' ceiling)	Fuji TV Studios Tokyo, Japan 9/21/80	1 minute, 33 seconds
Outdoor Time Aloft	Ken Blackburn Raleigh, NC 11/29/83	16.89 seconds

Paper Airplane Books

Paper Flight
by Jack Botermans
Holt, Rinehart & Winston, New York
$9.95

Paper Airplanes
20 aircraft to color, fold, & fly
by Marc Arceneaux
Troubador Press, Inc., San Francisco
$3.95

Flying Origami
by Eiji Nakamura
Kodansha International/
Harper & Row, Publishers, New York
$7.95

How To Make & Fly Paper Airplanes
by Captain Ralph S. Barnaby
Bantam Books, New York
$.75

The Great International Paper Airplane Book
by Jerry Mander, George Dippel and Howard Gossage
Simon and Schuster, New York
$8.95

30 Planes for the Paper Pilot
by Peter Vollheim
Wallaby Books, Pocket Books, New York
$8.95

Wings and Things
by Stephen Weiss
St. Martin's Press, New York
$8.95

Cut and Assemble Paper Airplanes that Fly
by Arthur Baker
Dover Books, New York
$3.95

The Paper Airplane Book
by Seymour Simon
Penguin Books, New York
$3.50

The Ultimate Paper Airplane
by Richard Kline
Simon and Schuster, New York
$6.95

The Best Paper Aircraft
by Campbell Morris
The Putnam Publishing Group, New York
$4.95

Collection of High Performance Paper Planes
(7 volume series, published in Japanese)
by Yasuaki Ninomiya
Seibundo-Shinkosha Publishing Co., Japan
$6.75 per volume

Paper Aircraft
(2 volume series, published in Japanese)
by Tatuo Yoshida
Privately published

Paper Airplane Kits

The Great International Paper Airplane Construction Kit
by Neosoft, Inc.
Simon and Schuster, New York
$39.95
Various versions of the contest designs, on Macintosh computer disk

Whitewings Paper Airplane Kits

Racer Sky Cub	$ 1.89
Twin Comets	$ 1.89
Prop Liner	$ 1.89
15-model Pro Series Kit	$12.00

The ultimate in hand-launch and catapult flight. Kits include pre-cut parts, Whitewings fiber airfoil paper, nontoxic glue, easy assembly and flight instructions. Available at retail outlets.

Jack Armstrong Card Kits
Tru-flite Models
PO Box 62
Roseville, MI 48066
$2.50
Paper construction kits of 14 famous World War II airplanes contain parts and assembly instructions. Also available in many air museum shops.

Flying Paper Scale Models
FPS Models
Box 269
Glen Ellyn, IL 60138
$3.95
World War II planes, reproduced to scale. Two models available with parts and complete instructions.

Whitewings Paper

The three sheets following this page are of Japanese Whitewings paper, specially recommended for building high-performance designs and competition paper airplanes. We recommend that you do not remove it from the book or start building planes with it until you have carefully read the introduction to Chapter Four. You may want to practice your design with other materials before building it with this paper. For best results, note carefully the orientation of the paper when laying out your design.